P9-BYF-166

Advance praise for *The Dog Whisperer*

"This wonderful book will help break the cycle of animal suffering caused by wrong-mindedness and harmful training methods. Paul Owens' nonviolent process will help prevent dogs from developing various behavioral and psychological problems, which can be difficult to treat later in life. It also helps us develop our empathy and understanding making us more humane—and more human—and thus more deserving of the company of dogs whose virtues we so often fail to live up to."

—From the Foreword by Dr. Michael W. Fox
Senior Scholar, Bioethics
The Human Society of the United States, Washington, D.C.

"Paul Owens has done dogs and dog lovers a real favor. He has given dog lovers permission to be kind, and as a consequence helped them to become more humane. He has given the dogs the chance to escape the brutal techniques that are so often imposed upon them 'for their own good.' This book provides us with a much needed modern reminder of the value of individual compassion, and shows us that love and learning can be fun and that they don't have to hurt."

—Karen L. Overall, M.A., V.M.D., PhD
Diplomate, American College of Veterinary Behaviorists
ABS Certified Applied Animal Behaviorist

"I enjoyed this book immensely. Paul Owens reveals the mystique of the dog and that unique bond we all strive to share with our precious canine pets. While other trainers snap, crackle, and pop, Paul creates an atmosphere of social cooperation. Everyone should enjoy *The Dog Whisperer*."

—William Campbell, BehavioRx Systems
Author, *Behavior Problems in Dogs*
and *Better Behavior in Dogs*

"After working for years to expose trainers' cruelty to animals in the production of movies, I applaud a book that encourages the compassion and nonviolence that dogs so richly deserve."

—Bob Barker, Host
The Price is Right

"How refreshing. Paul Owens offers us a well-thought-out, enjoyable, holistic text, which always has the physical and mental well-being of dogs at its heart. And, as an added bonus, *The Dog Whisperer* has many useful tips to promote the physical and mental well-being of dogs' human companions."

—Dr. Ian Dunbar
Author, Dog Behavior and founder, Association of Pet Dog Trainers

"*The Dog Whisperer* delivers a big message. With easy-to-follow lessons Paul Owens guides pet owners in raising cooperative, happy dogs. His techniques involve motivation rather than force. Well done, Paul. Your book leads the way to a better relationship with dogs."

—Terry Ryan
Author, *The Toolbox for Remodeling Problem Behaviors*

"This book is a must read for all dog lovers. Paul Owens offers a practical, heart-based approach to dog training filled with joy and love."

—Allen Schoen, D.V.M.
Author, *Love, Miracles and Animal Healing*

"Lately dog owners have become aware of the superiority of training systems based on kindness rather than harsh corrections. *The Dog Whisperer* shows them a very effective method that works everywhere, not just in the owner's backyard. It also offers guidance for the owners themselves. This enables the owner to achieve the balance in their own life that allows the deepest bonding with their dogs. I recommend this book to anyone who has ever had problems training their dog and to anyone who wants to learn the best way to train their dog."

—Nancy Scanlon, D.V.M.
Holistic Veterinarian

"Having worked with animals as a professional trainer over many years, I well understand the importance of changing human attitudes. Now, this book has changed my behavior. It has reminded me of many things I already knew but had somewhat lost touch with. Simply put, as I continue working with animals, including my own dog, I am having a lot more fun!"

—Mollie Hogan, Executive Director
Wildworks Wild Animals Nature Care Center
Topanga Canyon, California

"Paul's teaching methods adapt to working with schools, veterinarians, pet owners, and animals, creating order out of seemingly uncontrollable situations."

—Nancy Disbro, D.V.M.

"In the name of countless animals, thank you for your optimism and vision."

—Brian Forsgren, D.V.M.

THE DOG WHISPERER

A Compassionate, Nonviolent Approach to Dog Training

Paul Owens
with Norma Eckroate

ADAMS MEDIA CORPORATION
Avon, Massachusetts

Copyright ©1999, Paul Owens and Norma Eckroate.
All rights reserved. This book, or parts thereof, may not be reproduced
in any form without permission from the publisher; exceptions are
made for brief excerpts used in published reviews.

Published by Adams Media, an F+W Publications Company
57 Littlefield Street, Avon, MA 02322. U.S.A.
www.adamsmedia.com

ISBN: 1-58062-203-8

Printed in Canada.

J

Library of Congress Cataloging-in-Publication Data
Owens, Paul.
The dog whisperer: a compassionate, nonviolent approach to dog training/
by Paul Owens and Norma Eckroate.
p.   cm.
ISBN 1-58062-203-8
1. Dogs—Training. 2. Dogs—Behavior. 3. Human-animal communication.
I. Eckroate, Norma. II. Title.
SF431.0866   1999
636.7'0887—dc21   99-15824
CIP

The information in this book is not intended as a substitute for consulting a professional dog trainer or veterinarian. The advice it contains is general, not specific, and neither the authors nor the publishers can be held responsible for any adverse reaction to the suggestions, instructions, or recipes contained herein. Any attempt to train a dog that shows aggressive tendencies should be done under the supervision and guidance of a professional dog trainer.

This publication is designed to provide accurate and authoritative information with regard to the subject matter covered. It is sold with the understanding that the publisher is not engaged in rendering legal, accounting, or other professional advice. If legal advice or other expert assistance is required, the services of a competent professional person should be sought.
— From a *Declaration of Principles* jointly adopted by a Committee of the American, Bar
Association and a Committee of Publishers and Associations

Cover photograph by FPG International/Michael Malyszko.

Illustrations on pages 6, 142, and 145 by Aris Kakkis.
Illustrations of The Professor on page 142 and Betty on page 145 by Jacci Stincic.
Illustration of the Gentle Leader head collar on page 123 used with permission of Premier Pet Products.
All photos by Harvey Branman of Photography as an Art, Burbank, California, except photos on pages
133 and 134 by Tara Olsen and photo on page 68 by Sharon Eide.

This book is available at quantity discounts for bulk purchases.
For information, call 1-800-872-5627.

This book is dedicated to my Mother.

P.O.

Table of Contents

PART I: The Basics of Dog Training

PART II: The Lessons

PART III: Dealing with Problem Behaviors

Appendices:

Acknowledgments

Years ago, my great friend Jane Holland taught me about the "expanding heart." She said, "Just when you think your heart is so full of love that you can't possibly conceive loving more than you do, your heart expands. And it keeps on expanding until you come to the realization that love is infinite." And that is how I feel about all those who made this book possible.

For inspiration and her infinite and truly divine support, my sincere thanks and all my love goes to my twin sister, Pam. The same love and gratitude go to the rest of the Owens clan, Peg, Pat, Tom, and Ruth. A greater family hath no man.

For her unbelievable patience and enlightened gift of awareness coupled with her metaphysically astute way with words, I offer my deepest respect and appreciation to my coauthor, Norma Eckroate. Without her, it is doubtful this book would have appeared in this incarnational round.

To our agents, Lisa Hagan and Sandra Martin, thanks for your dogged pursuit and support. And to Jere Calmes and everyone at Adams Media, many thanks for your undying belief and conviction in this philosophy and work.

Heartfelt thanks go to my friends. It is truly an honor to be able to put your names in print for the world to see. I wish I had space to tell the story behind each name. As I write this, know that I am thinking of you individually and how special you are to me: Sister Donna Hawk; John and Carolyn Zenisek (go Joncar!); Holly Merriman; Linda, Lynley, and Stacy Turnbough; Arnie Richie; Bill Kennedy; Tim Leslie; Donna Estes; Maureen Williams; Helen Waldes; Robbin Herman; Fred and Gina Gloor; Carol Foster; Pat "you know who you are" Brooks; Rebecca Stack; Steve Hays; Elizabeth Walton; Bill, Mary, Cameron, and Murphy Needle; Tom McGuckin; Pat McGuckin; Tom and Cindy Fello; and Clay and Diane Williams.

For your supreme consideration and help in getting the words to match the thoughts, I wish to especially thank Marcie Goodman, Jane Malone, Robyn Polashuk, and, of course, my sister, the Sister, Pam.

To Michael W. Fox, D.V.M.; Nancy Disbro, V.M.D., Ph.D.; Marilyn McCort, D.V.M.; Brian Forsgren, D.V.M.; Ian Dunbar, Ph.D., MRCVS; and William E. Campbell: your work over the years with and for our beloved animals has truly been an inspiration. Thank you for your kindness, compassion, and dedication.

Special thanks go to Karen Overall, V.M.D, Ph.D.; Nancy Scanlon, D.V.M.; Mary Brennan, D.V.M.; Morgan Spector; Ken McCort; and Jerry Teplitz, Ph.D.; for their invaluable professional input, and to Jack Canfield for his "Soup-in-the Soul"–like assistance, and warmest regards and undying gratitude to Jim and Keelin O'Neill for their generosity and professional support.

To Jacci Stincic for her wonderful illustrations and Aris Kakkis for his brilliant creativity in translating thought to visual accessibility, thank you both so much. Special thanks to Harvey Branman at Photography as an Art in Burbank, California, for his friendship and outstanding photography. Thanks also to Tara Olsen for her excellent photography and her dog, the super model, Lucy.

Finally, to those friends with their furry sidekicks, a great big wag of my tail and scratch behind your ear! You made it all possible: Nichola Ellis with the irrepressible Conner and Tyson; Claudia Madrid with the ever-bounding Emily; Rosanna Lyons and the "I never met a human I didn't like" Angus; Renate Pless and "Mr. Energy" Joseph; the Williams family and the wonder Weimaraners, Jackson and Spalding; Holly Merriman and Marble (cake); the beautiful and very generous Leah Meyer; Tom O. and "If that's a water puddle, I'm not moving" Thunder; Robin Rosay and Merlin "the Merlinator"; Jane Malone and Orbit, the Queen of the Universe; Wendy Parrish and Judah. Thank you all so very much.

And, finally, to four of the greatest representatives of love ever incarnated in furry form, Tara and Molly, Sid and Charisse.

Foreword

It is simply not necessary to break an animal's spirit in order to live together in harmony. The old methods of training dogs and other animals by controlling them through domination—in a misguided desire for "absolute obedience"— foster an attitude of human superiority and justified violence, rather than kinship and mutual respect. I believe it is harmful for all of us, and especially for children, to observe and take part in such methods. Fortunately, these ways are becoming a thing of the past as they are now being challenged by less harmful methods of establishing control.

In looking at our relationship with animals, it's helpful to consider how wild animals relate to people. If a person suddenly came face to face with an animal and found himself in the animal's "personal space," the animal might panic and flee, become catatonic and play dead, or turn and attack. In all too many cases, those wild animals who are captured are at the mercy of a trainer whose methods—which include the chaining and beating of elephants and the roping and casting of horses—eventually break his spirit. Finally, the animal reaches a state of conditioned helplessness. In time the animal actually attaches himself to the trainer, who not only provides occasional relief from the beatings, but also represents his source of food, water, and security. Tragically, the animal learns to seek relief and solicit attention from the very trainer who abuses him.

We must ask ourselves, do the ends justify the means? When children and their parents applaud circus animal performances, they are not aware of the violent training methods that many of these animals have suffered through. Such training puts limitations on the human spirit and potential, just as it does on the animal's. Can any end justify breaking an animal's spirit?

Now we are entering a more empathic age and compassionate stage. As people mature, they desire a mutually enhancing relationship with their partners, one of kindness and respect. Likewise, we look for ways to educate our animals with compassion and love, in order to establish a relationship and bond based on mutual affection, understanding, and trust. Much skill, patience, and understanding are needed with animals to establish this bond.

Dogs have been domesticated for over 100,000 years and the domestication process has resulted in most of them losing their "wildness," which includes a high level of vigilance and fear of strangers and unfamiliar places and stimuli. This is one reason why dogs are easier to train than wolves, as I detail in my book, *The Soul of the Wolf.* This process of domestication manifests in the readiness of pups to bond with their caretakers or "parent-pack leaders" during their formative early weeks. During this critical period, between the ages of about five to ten weeks, pups develop their primary social attachments. In the wild it would be to their littermates, mother, father, and other pack members. In the domestic environment pups attach instead to their human family. It is on the basis of this attachment early in life that dogs are naturally amenable to nonviolent training.

This book by Paul Owens with Norma Eckroate is at the opposite end of the old-school moral spectrum and makes the nonviolent way of training a shoe-in. This book is as much about dog-human *education* as it is about dog training. It advocates educating our dogs with affection and understanding. Paul Owens helps us open up to dogs and relinquish control so dogs can actually educate, or "train," us to understand their ways, their needs, and their language.

This wonderful book will help break the cycle of animal suffering caused by wrong-mindedness and harmful training methods. Owens's nonviolent process will help prevent dogs from developing various behavioral and psychological problems, which can be difficult to treat later in life. It also helps us develop our empathy and understanding, making us more humane—and more human—and thus more deserving of the company of dogs whose virtues we so often fail to live up to.

—DR. MICHAEL W. FOX
SENIOR SCHOLAR, BIOETHICS
THE HUMANE SOCIETY OF THE UNITED STATES
WASHINGTON, D.C.

Preface

Years ago a friend of mine, a priest actually, suggested that I write a book about Jesus's dog. That idea began to percolate. It's hard to imagine Jesus or Buddha or Krishna or Moses "owning" a dog. But I'm sure at least a few four-legged furry personalities could be found hanging around the throngs. So how would an Enlightened One—a person who lives a truly conscious life—deal with a dog trying to steal a loaf of bread or a fish? "Sit, you miserable cur!" doesn't seem very likely. Nor can I imagine one of these people swatting the dog on the nose with a scroll. But, would he simply let the dog eat the stolen tidbit? And how would he train the dog? Maybe telepathy? I can just imagine Buddha under the bodhi tree or Jesus on the mount saying, "Nothing up my sleeve. For my next trick, I will stand behind this tree and, using just my mind, I will send my dog, Sparkus, visual images. He will roll over, get up, and go fetch my sandals."

Most of us, at one time or another, have thought or willed something and voilà, it happened. We have all had moments in our lives in which we felt consciously connected to the universe. I believe it is in these moments that intuition, creativity, and productivity flow. My first experience of this connectedness to the universe occurred when I was seven years old. Somewhere in the night I awoke to a half-asleep, half-awake consciousness. It felt like I was in a dream and watching it at the same time. Suddenly my body seemed to be frozen. I was lying on my back; my eyes, though closed, looked upward. I felt a split second tingle and then I exploded. A tremendous flash of incredible white light burst within my body. Every pore seemed to expand and grow. The light flooded my entire room and expanded outward.

Suddenly I felt whole and connected to absolutely everything. And everything was love. Unbelievable, unconditional, infinite love. In that microsecond of time, there were no questions, there were no answers. Everything was perfect as it was. After a period of time—I don't know how long—I fell into a deep sleep. Later, I woke up again. I was in tears. All I felt was gratitude. The experience of infinite, unbridled joy left me wanting everyone to experience it. And that is what I prayed for until I fell asleep again. It was a tremendously sweet sleep—every molecule of my body could taste it. The next day I couldn't think of anything else and I couldn't wait to go to sleep that night. Life was wonderful. I've been blessed with many other wonderful experiences since then, but this childhood taste of unconditional love was the ultimate. This was all.

Many years passed until I found someone who could explain what had happened to me that night, which I simply refer to as the "light of love." Since then I've had my ups and downs like everybody else. This one experience of "connectedness" didn't lead to a life free of problems. However, as one great teacher said, "Pain is a prod to remembrance." Now when I look back at the most challenging moments in my life, I realize the support has always been there any many times animals were providing that support. Even in the most troubling times, it was a matter of holding on and continuing to strive until light shone through once again.

I had been training dogs for many years using "standard" methods. But, as I share in Chapter 1, about ten years ago I had a sudden intuitive awareness that irrevocably changed my life. It's as if that long-ago "light of love" experience had planted a seed in my consciousness, which finally sprouted. A new sensitivity toward life had bloomed.

I could simply no longer jerk or "pop" a dog's leash to "remind" him of what he was or wasn't supposed to do. Nor could I yell to get my point across. I had come to a crossroad—a fork in the road between nonviolent and violent training. One path says, "My dog knows this, he's just being stubborn." And here's where the jerking, shocking, shaking methods are employed. The other says, if your dog doesn't understand what you're asking her to do, go back to the point where she was successful and, with compassion and understanding, start over again.

And that brings us to this book. The message of this book is not that nonviolent dog training is a new, groundbreaking path to enlightenment. But, I believe, like any life study, it can be a part of a journey toward wholeness. I truly believe, as we become more and more enlightened, both individually and as a species, we increase our capacity to love. And with increased empathy and compassion, the principles behind the learning process unfold naturally. It is our capacity to love that opens the doors to the evolution of our intelligence, not the other way around.

This book is a tad unique in that it adheres to the philosophy that the result of training your dog to sit is not as important as the process you take in getting her to do it. It's the "whys" and "hows"—the methods we use to train our dogs—that distinguish us as compassionate and loving beings. With this in mind, this book attempts to link intuitive and scientific methodology, all under the spiritual vehicle of nonviolence.

Now for a few practical matters: Part I of this book deals with the practical aspects of raising and training a dog, while Part II takes you through lessons divided into levels that progress from beginning to more advanced training. Finally, in Part III, you'll learn how to use nonviolent methods to resolve problem behaviors.

These training methods include some terminology that may be unfamiliar. For example, I don't use the word "command," which infers that something negative will happen if the dog doesn't "perform." Instead, I believe raising a dog nonviolently involves *asking* for behaviors. We do this by giving signals, which infers rewards and choices.

The word "handler" is used occasionally in this book because it is difficult to come up with a term for a dog's person that would prove familiar yet respectful. "Owner" is absolutely unacceptable. "Human companion" seems cold and "human friend" or "partner" seems weird, though these more accurately reflect the feel of the book. "Handler" is also a bit distant and doesn't fit well, but I beg your indulgence for using it occasionally. In addition, the interspersion of genders for both humans and dogs was used throughout the book, using both "he" and "she." Hopefully it works okay.

Also, I have taken a bit of liberty with the use of the words "reward" and "aversive." Though not scientifically accurate, I use the word "reward" to indicate a positive reinforcement. The term "aversive" is used to include something *intensely* disliked by the dog. I realize the word "aversive" can include lesser dislikes, such as simply turning away from her if she's barking or taking a treat away if she moves before being asked. I have tried my best not to get hung up on terminology, while at the same time honoring the spirit of the language.

The methods presented here are not cold, scientific training lessons. They do, however, align with sound behavioral principles. Indeed, it is in the application of science, rooted in compassion and awareness, that spiritual and behavioral evolution takes place. In short, this book introduces an insight of how we can unite science and spirit in the process of training our dogs.

Thank you for your interest in raising and caring for dogs with non-violence. May the Light of Love, Joy, and Peace surround and keep you and your animal friends.

PART I
The Basics of Dog Training

chapter one

Nonviolence Works!

Training with Rewards

Within weeks after their birth, dogs know how to put their behinds on the floor (sit), lie down, stand, stay, bark and not bark, run and walk toward us (come), walk by our side (heel), and find things with their noses (track). We don't have to teach them any of this. All we have to do—mostly for safety purposes—is ask them to please inhibit their biting on certain objects, go to the bathroom outside, and do what they do naturally—run, dig, jump, bark—when and where we request.

Basically there are two ways to train an animal—with physical force and coercion, which is often aversive, or with rewards, which personifies kindness. It's the age-old idea of getting an animal to do something by using a stick or giving her a carrot. I tell people that the choice they have to make is to either jerk, hit, shock, and/or shake their dog to get the desired behaviors—or give her rewards. Which is more humane? This book is about using carrots—and praise, toys, massage, social interaction, play, affection—and more carrots.

The *process* we use to teach our dogs to sit is as important as the result. The training methods we use are important not only because of what we are doing to our dogs, but also because of what we are doing to ourselves as human beings.

Aversive training says to the dog, "Do this or something bad will happen to you." *Reward-based* training suggests the opposite, "Do this and something good will happen." The difference between the two types of training is the consequences that are involved. In reward-based dog training, fear, pain, force, and submission do not exist.

With aversive methods, you are taught to jerk, hit, shock, or shake the dog to correct him when he does something you *don't want* him to do. You also jerk, hit, shock, or shake him every time you *want* him to do something. Finally he does what you want him to do because he doesn't want to experience the pain and/or discomfort any more. Then you gradually reduce the number of times you jerk, shock, hit, or shake him because he starts "behaving."

Sometimes jerking on the leash is referred to by euphemisms such as *leash correction* or *jerk correction*. But a jerk on the leash is a jerk, no matter what you call it. If too much force is used, dogs can quickly learn to fear the training. If poorly timed, jerking communicates messages that have nothing to do with the dog's pulling or other "misbehavior" the handler is trying to correct. The result is confusion and frustration for both the dog and the handler. As a result, the frustration leads to anger and even more force is usually employed. It's a vicious cycle.

In addition, jerking can lead to neck and spinal damage—and even whiplash injuries and it also creates the potential for emotional trauma, which, of course, translates into even more behavioral problems. According to behaviorist William Campbell a jerk on the leash doesn't have to be forceful to inflict an injury to your dog. He says that tests indicate that even a normal jerk can inflict 15 pounds of concentrated shock at 33 feet per second to a dog's spine and throat. Campbell also quotes a landmark survey by Anders Hallgren in 1992 which revealed that 252 out of 400 dogs examined by a chiropractor had misaligned spines. Among the 252 with spinal problems, 65 percent of them also had behavior problems, while only 30 percent of the dogs without spinal injuries had behavior problems. Of the dogs in the survey that were labeled as aggressive or hyperactive, 78 percent had spinal problems.

While some training methods limit the use of aversive force to a jerk on the leash, I've seen and heard of cases in which extremely abusive training methods were used. They include hanging in the air by a choke collar until the dog actually passes out, holding the head under water to keep the dog from digging in a hole, rubbing the nose in excrement, kicking to hurry the dog along, hitting on the nose with a rubber hose, pinching the ear with a contraption that places the ear between a wooden dowel and a bottle cap, zapping the dog with electricity, and much worse.

The alternative—the choice that I advocate—is nonviolent training that uses rewards and gentle persuasion to get your dog to do what you want. For example, if you reward a dog every time you want him to do something, he'll start responding more and more to get the reward. That's what dogs do. Gradually you stop rewarding him every single time and, gradually, he'll continue doing what you want just on the chance that a reward is coming his way.

Think of it this way: If I gave you $10,000 every time you sat on a particular chair whenever you came over to my house, where would you sit? And how often would you be visiting me? To keep you motivated, I might decide to offer other great stuff from time to time, such as an expensive watch, tickets to the Super Bowl, or a vacation in Bermuda. Eventually you might decide it's really worthwhile visiting me and sitting on that particular chair. Even if I don't give you stuff you might decide you actually like my company because, besides being generous, I'm a great guy! So let's say I then start giving you something really great every second or third time you come over. Just the anticipation of a possible reward would keep you coming. After all, did you ever see a person in Las Vegas being forced to play a slot machine? In the end, the possibility of a reward is all that's needed to keep people coming back.

Read the Label and Follow the Directions

Dog training, as it is currently practiced by many, is turned upside down. The primary reason people train dogs is *to keep them from doing things that come naturally.* They want to keep their dogs from using their teeth. They want to keep them from running. They want to keep them from eliminating. They want to keep them from jumping, digging, and barking. It's like putting them in behavioral straitjackets. So what can we do? The goal is to create an environment to let our dogs simply be themselves within the framework of our lifestyle.

Why dogs do what they do never changes. They do what they do for one reason—because it's in their best interest. Getting a reward—praise, food, or freedom—is the payoff. Avoiding danger is a payoff too—like getting someone to stop hitting or jerking them if they "sit." Dogs learn to anticipate these consequences.

I believe that dog training in the next century will evolve more and more toward nonviolence as trainers do less and less physically to shape their dogs' behavior. The key is harnessing your will power and channeling it through specific nonviolent training techniques. The greatest behavioral results are obtained when your will power is manifested in measured movements. This book explains how to do just that. Once the commitment is made, all you need to do is read the description and follow the directions on the label.

ILLUSTRATION 1

Please Read Label Before Adopting and Follow Directions

DOGGUS FRIENDLIUS

I pee, poop, chase, jump, dig, bark, and bite.
Assembly (training) required.
Batteries (food) not included.
Health care mandatory.
Yearly Cost: $750 to $3,000.

Additional Recommendations:
I prefer to sleep in the bedroom with you. Please provide a minimum of 2 hours a day of play, exercise, socialization, and employment. Education must include emotional, mental, and physical stimulation.

Benefits:
I will accept you as you are, unconditionally love you, work with you, grow with you, and together we will form a living, loving bond.

My Personal Journey to Nonviolent Dog Training

I remember the first time I correlated dog training with the concept of violence. I had been studying yoga in India and had not trained dogs in quite a while. One day the next-door neighbors adopted a new puppy, which they named Raju. They put her in the backyard where she began to bark and whine incessantly. Periodically the husband or wife would poke a head out the back door and scream at the pup to shut up. When the barking and whining continued, they would charge out the door and jerk on her leash. Raju would eventually stop and they would go back inside, slamming the door in frustration behind them. Soon the whole noisy cycle of barking, yelling, jerking the leash, and going in and out of the house began again, with both dog and human emotions escalating in intensity.

A few days passed and I finally decided enough was enough. The poor puppy's barking was quickly becoming a neighborhood noise nuisance. I felt compassion for the animal as well as the humans involved. It seemed time to put my experience as a dog trainer to good use. In addition, it occurred to me that several aspects of my yoga studies might be used to help in this situation. After all, there are many similarities between the learning principles that work for humans and those that work for dogs.

So I went next door and talked to the family. I explained that the puppy was barking because she didn't have anything else to do and pointed out that, as dogs are social animals, she needed companionship. I suggested they bring her into the house so she could be with the family. They did so and, lo and behold, with the addition of a few other socialization exercises and training tips, the barking decreased to a tolerable level. And, of course, both the puppy and her humans benefited from the budding familial bond.

It was a relatively easy process. A compassionate, nonviolent approach, along with the integration of some holistic perspectives, had benefited the puppy, her family, and, in fact, the whole neighborhood. I realized how different this episode was from the methods I had been taught long ago to get a dog to stop barking—such as yelling and threatening, pounding on the cage, and jerking on the leash. In retrospect, some of the methods I had been taught now seemed downright violent.

On my return to the United States, my brother Tom adopted a young dog from a shelter and asked for my help in training her. Her name was Thunder. In the first session with Thunder, I jerked her leash to get her attention. It was nothing serious—just a kind of "pay attention" pop on the leash. This sweet, sensitive animal put her ears back, turned her head, licked her lips, and did everything she could to say, "Okay, I submit. Please don't do that again." In a flash a shock ran through my body and a realization hit me. How quickly I had forgotten my experience in India. Without thinking, I had automatically used the primary method I had always used to "correct" a dog.

What was I doing? I suddenly knew that an animal could be harmed when the collar is jerked but also that, in a less overt way, I could even be harming myself in the process. A window had opened and common sense came rushing up through my awareness, "Duh—it's never necessary to jerk a leash to shape behavior, Paul." Common sense just isn't so "common" sometimes. In spite of having trained thousands of dogs and received numerous awards in competitive obedience, from that moment on I irrevocably knew that the training methods I had always used were wrong for me. That episode began a new journey. Thousands of people have come through my classes since then. In many cases they have expressed the same relief I felt to know there is another way—a nonviolent way—to get their dogs to do what they ask of them.

The good news is that nonaversive dog training is becoming more popular. However, it is estimated that only 20 percent of professional dog trainers in the United States teach strictly nonaversive methods of dog training. Most trainers use a combination of both aversive methods and reward-based methods. That means there are about forty million dogs in the country that are still being subjected to human violence as part of the training process. The point is, the majority of the population simply doesn't know that nonviolent training methods are available.

Taking the Lead in a Gentle, Empowering Way

Nonviolent dog training allows you to create a partnership with your dog using gentle persuasion based in kindness, respect, and compassion. This gentle persuasion is what nonviolent dog training is all about. In this method you use a gentleness with a flexible yet noncompromising attitude. The spoken word is actually full of power—and part of this power is based in the silence before, after, and between the spoken words.

Throughout history there have been many leaders who have eloquently expressed the power of gentle persuasion, including St. Francis of Assisi, Mahatma Gandhi, and Martin Luther King, Jr. One of my favorite examples comes from the plant world. The famous botanist Luther Burbank was the first to develop a cactus without thorns. He told the great yogi Paramahansa Yogananda how he did it: "I often talked to the plants to create a vibration of love. 'You have nothing to fear,' I would tell them. 'You don't need your defensive thorns. I will protect you.' "[1]

Nonviolence is not a new concept, but it is now taking root at a deeper level than ever before. Just as it is no longer acceptable to many people to punish a child by spanking, so, too, we are evolving as a species to eliminate violence in other areas. For many years there has been a movement toward the use of nonviolent, "cruelty free" products—such as cosmetics that do not include animal products or involve animal testing. Now it is time to totally eliminate violence in the training of dogs and other animals.

Today many people are familiar with the concept of nonviolent animal training because of the success of the book *The Man Who Listens to Horses,* the bestselling biography of Monty Roberts. Roberts belongs to a lineage of animal trainers, going back to "horse whisperer" John Rarey in the mid-nineteenth century. Instead of "breaking" wild horses, these trainers use approaches in which the horse voluntarily decides to work with them.

Gentler, kinder, and less dominating methods of animal training have also been used for several decades to train dolphins, killer whales, elephants, and other animals. Karen Pryor was one of the pioneers in training marine mammals. Later, she incorporated nonviolent approaches in the training of other animals, including dogs, which she details in her groundbreaking book *Don't Shoot the Dog.*

Pryor is one of a number of behaviorists who have shown us new ways to shape dog behaviors. A treat, a toy, or a scratch behind the ears, coupled with patience and consistency, and—voilà—behavioral

---

[1] Yogananda, Paramahansa, *Autobiography of a Yogi,* Self-Realization Fellowship, 1946, page 411.

success. The point of this book is that we humans have an equal role in the behavioral give-and-take equation. The fact that we can get a dog to sit or lie down when we ask is not the entire picture. In this philosophy, which is certainly not new, how we go about it is equally important. Our desire to elicit behavioral responses that correspond to our limited view of what is right, wrong, or simply appropriate doesn't justify violent methodology. The end never justifies the means. And might does not make right.

Responding Versus Reacting to Your Dog

Sometimes all that is necessary to tilt the scales toward nonviolence during training is simply to become aware of the obvious. A few years ago a couple called me to do a consultation for a dog that was exhibiting aggressive behavior. When I arrived at the home, Lucky was locked in the basement. I learned the wife was a psychiatrist and the husband was a psychologist. This couple knew more about operant and classical conditioning than I could ever hope to know in this lifetime. Yet, there I was setting up a behavior modification program for them and their dog, which was, in principle, similar to the ones they design and implement every day of the week for human beings! Fortunately the light bulb went off in their heads and they quickly realized they had not been using their expertise with their own dog. They were able to implement my suggestions with great results. A few weeks later when I checked back, Lucky was well on her way to becoming a well-mannered member of society.

Like this couple, all of us have blocks in our awareness. It's as if we sometimes forget to "connect the dots." Often it's just a matter of finding the trigger to release and remember what we already know. To do this, we have to pause before we act and learn to *respond* rather than *react*. "Reacting" denotes an emotionally based knee-jerk behavior to a particular situation. On the other hand, a "response" means we bring all of our wisdom, creativity, intuition, and emotion to the situation. Why learn to respond rather than react? For one thing, when you stop and consider what you are about to do with your dog, you are able to focus on how to deal with the problem rather than the symptom.

Let's say a dog is barking at the mail carrier walking toward the house. The knee-jerk reaction is to respond to the symptom, which is the barking, rather than the cause. Most people never think about what is causing the dog to bark; he might be excited, he might be afraid, he might simply be saying hello. In essence, he perceives that he's doing his job. In most cases, people deal with the barking by yelling at the dog, hitting him with a newspaper, or jerking him on the leash to get him to stop. Regardless of the reason the dog was initially barking, he now associates the mail carrier walking toward him as a danger because of the bad things that happened to him when he barked at that person. So now the dog has a growing aggression problem toward people in uniforms approaching the house. Imagine, on the other hand, if every time the mail carrier showed up and the dog started barking, you interrupted him with a phrase like "Who's that?" and then gave him a treat. You will have ended the barking and the dog will have associated the mail carrier with something positive. So, by using this nonviolent, positive approach, you've stopped the barking and, in the process, you've made the dog more social.

Every dog deserves respect. And that respect includes being considerate. You should do your best to find out why a dog is doing what he is doing before responding. Otherwise, it is easy to inadvertently fly off the handle and react in a way that might harm the dog and actually compound the behavioral problem. Reacting blocks respect; responding fosters respect.

Consideration also includes the recognition that every dog learns at his or her own rate. People often ask me how long it takes to train a dog. The answer is—it takes as long as it takes. In many ways, training a dog is like raising a child. No parent would ever expect a child to learn to behave perfectly within three months or six months or even three years. Yet many people expect a dog to learn to sit or walk by their side reliably with just a few days' training or after only a few sessions. It just doesn't happen that way.

What Is Violence?

Everyone looks at the world differently. And we look at dogs differently. To many of us a dog is a loved, cherished being with her own distinct personality. Our dogs are members of our families and our partners in life. They teach us patience and love and allow us to see these qualities reflected back when we look at them. Yes, to some, dogs are mirrors of our most exemplary human characteristics. Their presence increases our feelings of self-worth and helps to heal us emotionally and physically. In their role as service dogs, they help us stand and see, both figuratively and literally. They tell us when the phone is ringing or when someone is at the door. They predict epileptic seizures and can even smell diseases—and so much more.

To others, a dog is an extension of *machismo*; if a dog is big, tough, and mean, it must mean that the dog's owner is that way too. Finally, in some people's eyes, dogs are simply possessions, which are disposable. Many people give up on dogs with behavior problems such as eliminating in the house or excessive barking, and drop them off at the shelter. In the United States alone, desensitization, ignorance, and superstition are significant causes of more than four million dogs being put to death annually—not to mention the cruelty and the suffering of countless others.

People have dropped out of my classes because, as one guy put it, "I need to work with a more 'hands-on' approach." Read "jerk and shake" in that comment. "He's a rottweiler," another guy said after punching his dog in the face. "He can take it." I then reported the man for this abuse. I felt sorry for the poor dog.

Violence is any behavior or thought that is harmful and stops growth—emotionally, physically, and mentally. Nonviolence is the opposite—any behavior or thought that promotes and fosters self-awareness, health, growth, and safety in these areas. All dogs are individuals with their own unique personalities just like humans. And every situation in which a dog and a human interact is unique for that time and place. It is up to each one of us to determine what is violent and what is not at that moment in time. This holds true for behavior directed toward animals, the environment, and, as common sense dictates, ourselves. It takes lots of practice.

Here are some examples, a frame of mind, to clarify the differences and help you draw the nonviolence/violence line in the sand. To interrupt a dog that is climbing on the dining room table or chewing an electric cord, you can distract him with sound and motion and ask him to do something else. Can you see the difference between interrupting him and frightening him? In the same vein, you can encourage your dog or you can force and intimidate him by jerking, hitting, shocking, or shaking. You can create an environment where your dog learns by his successes or you can punish him. Does that mean there is no anger in the training of dogs? Let's face it, we're human beings and anger is a human emotion. Every now and then we humans get angry.

But there is a difference between ethical anger and violent anger. Ethical anger is anger in which emotion is expressed appropriately and with full awareness of the consequences of that expression. It means expressing oneself without causing harm. In its best expression, anger is a prod to positive change. Violent anger has no regard for consequence. At those rare times when you find yourself angry, reward-based dog training takes the violence out of that anger. This means that in no situation whatsoever do you ever harm your dog. And that takes awareness.

A nonviolent approach doesn't victimize. It is a proactive approach in which the nonviolent principles of love, respect, and compassion are foremost in your mind. A nonviolent approach also means not taking on the role of a victim, although there are times when we must put ourselves in harm's way to protect or care for a loved one or for a greater good. For example, Gandhi practiced what he called peaceful resistance in India's struggle for independence. The point is, a commitment to nonviolence doesn't preclude using our good old common sense, as well as wisdom, humor, and other nonaversive conflict resolution methods. We are the intelligent, compassionate, intuitive, creative species, are we not? Certainly we can figure out how to shape a dog's behavior without the use of aversive methods.

Aversive training methods are not only harmful to animals; I believe they are at least part of the reason that animals sometimes exhibit violent behavior toward humans. According to recent statistics, there were 4.5 million dog bites in the United States last year and 75 percent of the victims were children. In fact, dog bites are the leading cause of children being taken to the hospital.

The Cycle of Violence

So, why do people still continue to harm or threaten to harm their dogs? There are three major reasons: (1) it's always been done this way, (2) the sense or need of the person to be in physical control of a situation, or (3) wanting to punish the dog. If a person is using aversive methods with a dog because "it's always been done this way," habituation and familiarity have set in. Changing things can be a threat to the status quo. To less secure individuals it also might mean that they would have to admit they had been violent in the past. This would be like looking in a mirror and seeing themselves as different from who they thought they were. Scary! The other reasons people continue to use harmful training methods—their need to be in physical control and wanting to punish the dog—are usually associated with anger and frustration. As I said earlier, anger has no place in dog training. It shuts off and restricts wisdom, creativity, and intuition. Both the person and the dog suffer. To quote from the sacred text, the *Bhagavad-Gita*: "From unfulfilled desire comes frustration; from frustration, anger; from anger, ruin."

The tendency to use aversive techniques—violent force or the threat of force—is ingrained early in life. For example, whenever a child sees another person demonstrating brutish behavior, she learns that we "win" by being bigger, stronger, and tougher. In nonviolent dog training there is no "winning" because there is no competition.

When we use aversive training methods instead of nonviolent alternatives, we risk ensnaring our dogs and ourselves in a downward spiral of aggression and we desensitize ourselves to the higher aspects of who we are as humans. There was a recent article in a newspaper about a fourteen-year-old girl who had just killed a deer for sport. An accompanying photo showed the dead animal strapped to the hood of her father's car. The girl was asked, "How did you feel when you killed the deer?" She said, "Well, when I killed my first one last year I felt pretty bad. Now it's easier and *I don't think about it at all"* (emphasis added). Education is the key to creating awareness.

Studies have shown that humans who are violent toward animals often extend that behavior and become violent toward other humans. In the last decade, a number of news headlines have repeated the same tragic facts in story after story—a child who exhibited violence toward animals had turned to murdering people.

Reward-based dog training, through its nonviolent approach, promotes compassion and encourages our true nature as sensitive, empathic, loving beings. It acts as a bridge and fosters human-to-animal and human-to-human *nonviolence*.

Dogs Are, Well, Dogs

In theory, training a dog is easy. You form an image in your mind, such as the dog in a sitting position, choose the appropriate training tools, and shape the behavior to match the picture in your head. It just takes time, patience, and a little bit of skill. And that's the rub. Many people don't take the time. Out come the choke, prong, and shock collars—and the jerking, hitting, kicking, shocking, shaking, and ear pinching. The message is "You'll do this *now* or else!"

Let's face it, dogs bite, they eliminate, they bark, and they jump. They are themselves. They are not morally good or bad. They are not guilty nor are they heroes. They just are. And we are still discovering the fullness of what that means. In recent years scientists have postulated that we humans use only 15 to 20 percent of our brain power. That's on a good day, I think. Given this human limitation, it seems arrogant and downright silly for us to think that we know all there is to know about dogs and their behavior.

This book offers a new approach to mainstream dog training by focusing on the training *process* as the actual goal. It is when you lose sight of the process as a goal that the invisible leash of your will power is weakened. Your training becomes unclear, imprecise, and poorly timed. When this happens your bond with your dog is also weakened and she is either confused about what you want her to do or the payoff just isn't big enough for her. In other words, your dog thinks, in essence, "Without motivation, why bother?"

As a species we humans have accomplished some amazing things. We've tapped into the intelligence and bravery to put a person on the moon. We've been inspired to create outstanding works of art, thrilling books, awe-inspiring movies, and songs of joy. We've developed the stamina and physical ability to run a marathon, lift a thousand pounds, and jump 8 feet in the air. And we've found the inexhaustible hope and faith to heal life-threatening illnesses. Certainly with all of these abilities, it is also possible for us to teach a dog to walk by our side without having to hit, kick, shock, shake, or jerk him.

The methods we choose to raise and train our dogs determine not only behavioral responses, they also shape our own emotional, physical, and intellectual growth. And they help to define and shape who we are as individuals and as a species. This book is a presentation of nonviolent partnering with your canine pal. The goal is to enable you to learn and grow together and to experience unbelievable joy. It all starts by addressing the concept of nonviolence: kindness, respect, compassion, responsibility, and love.

chapter two

The 9 Ingredients for Optimum Health and Growth

Overview of the 9 Ingredients

It was the philosophy of holistic health contained in the eight steps of an ancient school of thought called Raja Yoga that inspired me to formulate a model for the optimum care and training of dogs. Most disciplines have a set of rules, which, if followed with perseverance and effort, provide measurable results in physical, mental, and emotional growth. The "nine ingredients" of dog care fit right in. They are: a high quality diet, play, socialization, quiet time, exercise, employment, rest, step-by-step training, and health care.

When I present my *Nonviolence Works!* programs in elementary schools, I try to make the nine ingredients accessible to the students by teaching them a little poem:

Food and play and socialize,
Quiet time and exercise,
Give your dog a job to do
And lots of rest when day is through.
Train with love, respect, and care,
And see your vet throughout the year.

These nine ingredients comprise a holistic picture of all the factors that contribute to and influence your dog's behavior. Each of these ingredients is a piece of the puzzle needed to shape the environment in which optimal learning takes place. When you create an optimum learning environment, training is easier, it's quicker, and it's a more pleasant experience.

Think for a minute about your own requirements for optimum health. If you are tired, hungry, sick, or had a bad day at work, you simply aren't going to be at your best. This illustrates the value of looking at and modifying behavior from a "big picture" or holistic point of view. It is not only the quantity but also the quality of each ingredient that affects behavior.

When you incorporate all nine ingredients into your dog's life, a synergy develops. I love the concept of synergy. It occurs whenever the sum of the total is greater than the sum of the parts. In other words, it's like 2 + 2 + 2 equals 10 *or* 20 *or* 30 *or* 100. The result is greater than that which would have manifested if any one ingredient was applied singly or even when several of the ingredients are applied but others are missing. One example of synergy at work might include the Beatles—they were great individually, but as a unit, they were magnificent. The same goes for any championship sports team. Applications of great synergy in the dog world would include dog sled teams and animal-assisted therapy groups such as Delta Society's Pet Partners, which takes teams of humans and dogs into hospitals and nursing homes. In your home, this synergy is also at work. Scientific studies have proven that a person's well-being, both physically and emotionally, benefits from interaction with dogs and other animals. On the other side of the coin, it has also been proven that an animal's well-being is enhanced by positive human contact.

When you read about each of the nine ingredients, keep in mind that these ingredients are structured to make dog training easy and part of your everyday routine. Additionally, you will probably note that these are the same ingredients humans need to maintain health, happiness, safety, and growth. This whole philosophy is based upon pure common sense; it's just a matter of gently letting it flow into your daily lifestyle and routine. As a result, there's no sense of dread or weight of responsibility in *having* to train and care for your dog. It becomes a natural process of everyday living.

If your dog exhibits behavioral problems, I suggest taking a mental snapshot of all the aspects of your dog's life and then review each of these nine ingredients to determine which ones might be out of balance. Many behavioral problems just disappear when this nine-part holistic approach for optimum health and well-being becomes the focus. In addition, when all of these ingredients are provided in a balanced way, dogs are much easier to train. (Part III of this book deals with the most common problem behaviors. Some severe behavioral problems are beyond the scope of this book. If a problem persists, please call a professional dog trainer who is versed in nonviolent training methods. Remember, it's always better to err on the side of safety.)

Ingredient Number 1: A High Quality Diet

This section may include more than you want to know about your dog's diet. If that's the case, simply skip to the suggested diet recommendations:

🦴 *Option 1:* Canned food and/or kibble made from "human grade" ingredients (see page 25)

🦴 *Option 2:* Molly's Favorite Gourmet Dinner (see page 26)

🦴 *Option 3:* Homemade diet with all the options (see page 27)

"A dog is what she eats." I'm going on record here to say if a dog is genetically sound, there is really no reason most healthy dogs can't live to be twenty, even twenty-five years old. In fact, this is not unrealistic. Holistic veterinarian Nancy Scanlon, D.V.M., reports a recent case of a dog that lived to be twenty-seven. Today, the average dog's life span is ten to fifteen. I truly believe more and more dogs would live much longer if we integrated all of the nine ingredients—and it starts with good nutrition.

When I'm consulted about a particular behavioral problem, one of the first things I ask the client is about the dog's diet. A dog's diet can affect his mood, his overall health and stamina, and, of course, his life span. Behavioral problems can be related to a low quality diet, eating too much, eating too little, or food allergies or sensitivities.

Your dog's nutritional requirements depend on her age, breed, size, daily activity level, overall health, emotional make-up, physical sensitivities, and tolerances. I am spending more time on this subject than on most of the other nine ingredients because it is such a primary foundation of behavior.

Good nutrition for your dog is actually pretty easy to attain; however—to put it bluntly—not if you buy what Madison Avenue is selling. Unfortunately, although there are a few small companies that sell higher quality, more natural dog foods, most commercial dog foods available today are not as nutritious as the public is led to believe.

Most pet food companies want you to think their foods are "scientifically formulated," "completely balanced," and "100 percent nutritionally complete." The government allows these claims to be made based on feeding trials that are done for a limited period of time. The fact is, no one really knows the nutritional requirements of a cat or dog to the extent that those claims could possibly be valid.

Veterinarian Dr. R. L. Wysong argues that pet food companies should not be allowed to use the "100 percent complete" claim. He uses a human parallel as an analogy: "How many parents would take the advice of a pediatrician who placed a packaged food product on the exam table and told the parent that this is the only product they should feed the child day-in, day-out, for the child's lifetime, and further that they should be sure to not feed any other foods because that might unbalance the product? Even if the pediatrician gave assurances of nutrient analyses that exceeded required minimum levels, feeding trials, and even if the label guaranteed '100% complete and balanced,' how many parents would accept such counsel?"[1]

Of course, one of the main reasons we wouldn't buy into the idea that any single packaged food product is nutritionally adequate for a person is that it lacks the health-giving properties of food that is eaten closer to its natural state. The canning or drying process strips food of its life energy. We get the greatest benefit from food when it is in the freshest and most natural state.

Let's look at the problems with many commercial pet foods on the market today:

---

[1] Wysong, R.L., D.V.M., "The Myth of the 100% Complete Manufactured Diet," *Journal of the American Holistic Veterinary Medical Association*, February–April, 1992, vol. 11, no. 1, page 17.

Problem No. 1: Where's the raw food? Only raw food contains "life energy."

"Life energy" is a subtle but powerful aspect of food. It is present in all fresh raw food and, in its gross form, especially in beneficial bacteria and enzymes.

Beneficial bacteria are the "good" or friendly bacteria that are naturally present in the body. They are used for the digestion of food and they also help to suppress undesirable bacteria and yeast. Sometimes the body's own supply of beneficial bacteria is depleted. When this happens, the bad guys can multiply, creating an imbalance. To insure a plentiful supply of the "good guy" bacteria, beneficial bacteria can be added to the diet in supplement form. A number of natural pet products companies offer products specifically formulated for dogs that contain beneficial bacteria.

Enzymes are protein molecules that break down and digest our food. Without them, food is not properly digested; therefore, nutrients are not fully absorbed by the body and metabolic deficiencies can result. Enzymes are present in all raw foods, including raw meat. The body has its own stores of enzymes so when you, or your dog, eat enzyme-deficient food, the body must draw on its own enzyme reserves from organs and tissues. Research studies support a strong correlation between enzyme deficiency and diseases, both acute and chronic. You can overcome this problem by feeding your dog more raw foods, either mixed in with his usual food or as a treat, and you can also purchase enzyme supplements to add to his food. Several manufacturers market digestive enzymes for dogs; others include digestive enzymes in their dog supplement formulas. One of these products can be particularly helpful if your dog has a digestive problem, if he has been on a poor quality diet, or if he is getting on in years.

Life energy in its more subtle form deals with thought. For example, when a carrot is just a seed, it cannot sustain an animal. Picked at the optimum moment of growth, however, the carrot is a great source of vitamins and minerals. The growth process, which empowered it from seed to maturation, is life energy. There is a perfect moment for carrots to be pulled from the ground and eaten—the perfect moment of optimum health-giving properties. But what if you can't pick and eat a carrot at the perfect time? According to Eastern thought, humans are unique in that they can actually infuse this positive life energy *into* food. It's a matter of thinking good, healthy thoughts and willing those healthy thoughts into the food you are preparing or eating. Does this work? Some studies indicate that focused thoughts can be transmuted into health-giving medicine. Whenever you prepare food for yourself or your dog, imagine infusing the food with "life energy." This is really not so different from a belief in prayer or the power of a deity to heal. Whatever you believe, what have you got to lose?

Problem No. 2: Processing destroys nutrients.

In addition to the lack of beneficial bacteria and enzymes, there are other problems with food when it's processed. Whether it's canned, dry kibble, or semimoist, processing destroys a good deal of the nutritional value of the food. Of these three choices, canned food is the best because fewer nutrients are destroyed in the canning process than by the other methods. Most kibbles are low quality foods that have undergone more processing than canned foods. They are pressure cooked, flavored, colored, dehydrated, and then sprayed with fat to make them tasty. In addition to the loss of nutrients due to all of this processing, Alfred J. Plechner, D.V.M., says in his book *Pet Allergies* that he finds many animals have a food intolerance or allergy to kibble. He writes, "I believe the reason is because kibble is a concentrated collection of many of the foods that are the most allergenic for animals. Practically everything on my allergic HIT List is found in those sacks: beef, milk, wheat, corn, yeast, fish meal, plus a bountiful array of chemical additives. There's probably some mold, hair and other impurities in there as well."[2] All of that being said, there are some pet food manufacturers that have taken great effort in

---

[2] Plechner, Alfred J., D.V.M., and Martin Zucker, *Pet Allergies: Remedies for an Epidemic*, J.P. Enterprises, 1986, page 29.

producing the freshest, highest quality kibble possible. (See Appendix C for our suggestions.)

Semimoist foods are the poorest quality foods. They contain a large amount of artificial flavorings, preservatives, and sugars, which are required in order to keep them in an ever-moist state. Finally, in all processed foods, but particularly with most kibbles and in all semimoist foods, the protein is of low quality and difficult to digest. See the Appendix for natural pet food manufacturers that produce kibble of a higher quality.

Problem No. 3: Most commercial pet foods are made of low quality meats.

Most commercial dog foods don't contain "human quality" ingredients. That would be too expensive. Therefore, most pet food manufacturers use ingredients such as *meat by-products* that are not considered fit for human consumption. This is not just true of the grocery store brands; even some "premium" brands sold by veterinarians are not so premium when you know what they contain. In *The Natural Dog,* Mary L. Brennan, D.V.M., describes it this way: "The government standards actually allow by-products to include diseased chicken, beef, or pork; tankage from cooked or condemned carcasses; indigestible parts of carcasses such as ligaments, tendons, and cartilage; and parts of the animal you probably wouldn't consider as food at all, such as feathers, beaks, and hooves."[3] Yuck!

The U.S. government's term for these meats is "4-D," which stands for *dead, dying, diseased,* and *disabled.* Dr. Brennan says, "These by-products are considered acceptable for commercial pet foods because they have been processed at such high temperatures that they are considered sterile. Of course, processing at these temperatures also destroys many nutrients. (The pet food industry tries to compensate for this by adding isolated vitamins, minerals, and amino acids to make up for what was cooked away or missing in the first

[3] Brennan, Mary L., D.V.M., with Norma Eckroate, *The Natural Dog: A Complete Guide for Curing Owners,* Plume, 1994, pages 84–85.

place due to low quality ingredients.) In any event, I certainly wouldn't want to eat a cancerous tumor that the government calls 'safe' because it has been sterilized. Nor do I think pet foods that contain these ingredients are nutritious for our beloved companion animals."[4]

Problem No. 4: Some ingredients in many commercial foods are "not fit for human consumption."

Commercial pet foods often contain many other ingredients of the lowest quality, such as rancid or moldy grains, rancid oils, and other refuse from food processing plants that is not considered fit for human consumption. This includes the so-called natural flavor that is sprayed onto dry food. In reality, most companies use 4-D meat that has actually rotted (they called it fermented), then add phosphoric acid to stop the rotting process. Then it's sprayed onto dry food to make it tasty and appealing to dogs. In addition, pet food companies sometimes include other items you wouldn't consider to be food, such as hooves and feathers. Even peanut hulls have been added to food and labeled as "vegetable fiber."

Problem No. 5: Additives, flavor enhancers, chemical preservatives, and sugars are not good for Fido.

Many commercial pet foods also contain dyes, stabilizers, thickeners, "flavor enhancers," and chemical preservatives, such as sodium nitrite, sodium nitrate, butylated hydroyxanisole (BHA), butylated hydroxytoluene (BHT), monosodium glutamate (MSG), sodium metabisulfite, and ethoxyquin. Some of these preservatives, such as ethoxyquin and sodium nitrate, have been linked to cancer. These preservatives must be listed on the label if the pet food manufacturer adds them to the food. However, pet food manufacturers often buy ingredients that already contain preservatives such as ethoxyquin and, in those cases, are not required to list them on the label. Various forms of sugar, including corn syrup, and excessive salt are also added to the food to entice a dog to a particular food.

---

[4] Ibid., page 85.

If all of these facts about most commercial pet foods aren't enough, here's something else to consider. In her book, *Food Pets Die For*, Ann N. Martin discloses some disturbing research. Euthanized cats and dogs, including our beloved companion animals, are allowed in the category of "4-D" meat by-products, and some companies actually include them in their foods. I have no idea how widespread this practice is; however, according to Martin's research, some veterinarians and rendering plants say it is common, while pet food manufacturers vehemently deny it.

So . . . What Should You Feed Your Dog?

The very best diet for your dog is a homemade food made of organic ingredients, along with quality supplements. This means meats and other ingredients that are free of pesticides, antibiotics, and hormones. However, since time and money are prime considerations for many people, below you'll find several options to raise the nutritional bar. As I mentioned earlier, a number of factors determine your dog's unique nutritional requirements, including her age, breed, size, daily activity level, emotional make-up, physical sensitivities, and tolerances. Most veterinarians, like most medical doctors, have studied only rudimentary nutrition. Many veterinarians actually sell brands of food that contain questionable ingredients. A veterinarian who is trained in holistic modalities is more likely to be the one to help you tailor the highest quality diet.

Option 1: Canned food and/or kibble made from "human grade" ingredients

While homemade food, which I'll share in Options 2 and 3 that follow, is the absolute best, for most people it's just not feasible. So, the next best alternative is to find a canned food and/or kibble made by a manufacturer of natural pet food. (See Appendix C for my recommendations.) Then mix in a few of the raw food items and nutritional supplements listed on page 30 as "The Extras."

When selecting a commercial food, remember that even though a company advertises "all natural," its pet food may contain questionable ingredients. Short of visiting the pet food processing plant—and tracing the suppliers of meats, grains, and other ingredients—it is extremely difficult to judge the quality of manufactured pet foods. One indicator of a higher quality is the use of "human grade" meats that are labeled USDA (United States Department of Agriculture) and other human grade ingredients and no by-products. While very few companies use human grade ingredients, if a label or product brochure indicates this, you can be pretty sure the quality is much higher than other pet foods. Of course, it also means the food will be more expensive than other brands.

Remember, a canned food is always nutritionally superior to a dry kibble, however, as we mentioned earlier, there are high quality kibbles available from companies that use pure, natural ingredients. Many veterinarians believe that kibble has an additional benefit in that it helps to keep teeth clean, exercise the jaws, and promote the health of the gums. My dog Molly's diet consists of half canned food and half kibble and she just loves her daily treat of a nice big raw carrot that she holds between her paws while devouring. This proportion of half canned food and half kibble is preferable, but any amount of canned food is superior to none. (See Appendix C for recommended food manufacturers.)

Option 2: Molly's Favorite Gourmet Dinner
 2 cups water
 3/4 cup brown rice
 1-1/4 cups baked, cubed (1/4- to 1/2-inch cubes)
  organic free-range turkey
 1/4 cup raw grated zucchini
 1/4 cup lightly steamed broccoli (small pieces)
 1-1/2 teaspoons extra virgin olive oil
 Vitamin and mineral supplement (according to label
  directions)
 Enzyme supplement (according to label directions)

 1. Put the water into a pan along with the rice. Bring to a boil and then reduce heat to a simmer, cover, and cook

for 1-1/4 hours. You want it to be overcooked so it is more digestible for your dog.
2. Mix all of the ingredients and serve.

Option 3: Homemade diet with all the options
The following homemade diet is courtesy of Mary Brennan, D.V.M., and reprinted from her book *The Natural Dog*.[5] It is a good basic diet for adult dogs. To make homemade food for a puppy or a dog who is overweight, suffers from food allergies, or requires a restricted protein diet (such as kidney patients), refer to *The Natural Dog*.

I have chosen to reprint Dr. Brennan's diet because it gives you a lot of range to pick ingredients that you prefer or that your dog particularly likes. I suggest multiplying the indicated quantities to make large batches of the food. Then keep three or four days' supply in the refrigerator and freeze the rest. However, don't freeze more than three or four days' supply in any one container. Be sure to allow a day or so to defrost a container before you need it.

Be sure to serve the food at room temperature. The easiest way to do this is to put the food in the dog's bowl and then put that bowl in a larger bowl of hot water for ten to fifteen minutes. This is preferable to using a microwave since it would cook some of the nutrients out of the food while it is being heated.

You'll see that the meat portion of the mixture can be cooked in a couple of different ways. One method I recommend is to prepare chicken, for example, by simmering it in water in a pot on the stove. Then you can mix the cooking water in with the food and end up with a stew-like consistency that most dogs just love. So it is easily digestible, the grain should be overcooked. Use 2-1/2 cups of water for each cup of uncooked grain. Bring to a boil and then turn to a simmer, cover, and cook for 1-1/4 hours.

[5] Brennan and Eckroate, pages 100–102.

Grain	Use cooked brown rice, oats (usually in the form of oat-meal), corn, wheat berries, wheat bulgur, barley, rye, or millet. If you use oatmeal or corn, increase the amount to one-half more. Use rye as an alternative occasionally in either a cooked whole grain form or try crumbled rye crackers (buy the no-salt variety). (*Note:* Although brown rice is preferable to white rice, some dogs may suffer from digestive problems and do better on a mixture of half brown rice and half white rice until their systems get used to the extra bulk.)
Protein	Use boiled or broiled lean hamburger, chicken, turkey, or lamb. Choose lean meat with a little fat. Up to three times a week you can substitute one-half of the meat portion with cooked beans, lentils, or tofu, if desired. If using raw meat, you can minimize the possibility of harmful bacteria such as salmonella by making sure it is fresh and taking precautions in your care and handling of it.
Vegetable	Experiment to find the vegetables your dog likes best. Try grated raw zucchini, yellow squash, or carrots; chopped alfalfa sprouts; lightly steamed broccoli, asparagus (most dogs love it), corn, green beans, turnips, parsnips, or peas. Try other vegetables to see how your dog responds, but avoid onions and cabbage because they can cause digestive upsets. If your dog doesn't like the vegetables at first, try chopping them finely and mixing well into the food.
Oil	Choose any high-quality vegetable oil: safflower, corn, sesame, wheat germ, sunflower, flaxseed, or extra virgin olive oil. Or buy an oil supplement for pets from a natural pet food company. During the winter months give extra virgin olive oil or cod-liver oil a few times a week. *Note:* High-quality oils are cold pressed and should be refrigerated after opening. Wheat germ and flaxseed oil are extremely high in nutrients but turn rancid easily. These oils should be refrigerated as soon as you get them home—even before opening. Omega Nutrition manufactures a high-quality flaxseed oil that's an excellent source of the Omega 3 fatty acids.

Vitamin and Mineral Supplements	Choose a vitamin and mineral supplement formulated for dogs from a natural pet food company. Be sure it is made of natural whole food ingredients and contains no preservatives or artificial ingredients. Use according to directions on the label.
Enzyme Supplement for Dogs	Use according to directions on the label.
Antioxident Supplement for Dogs	Use according to directions on the label.

Fix-It-Yourself Basic Diet–Quantities: Use the following chart to determine how much food to make per day. Multiply these quantities to make food for more than one dog or to make more than one day's supply. Remember that each dog's metabolism differs and these are only approximate amounts.

Dog's Weight in Pounds	5	10	25	40	60	80
Grain	1/2 cup	1 cup	2 cups	2-1/2 cups	4 cups	5 cups
Protein	2-1/2 T.	1/3 cup	2/3 cup	1-1/8 cups	1-1/3 cups	1-3/4 cups
Vegetables	1 T.	1/8 cup	1/4 cup	1/3 cup	1/2 cup	2/3 cup
Oil	1/4 tsp.	1/2 tsp.	1 tsp.	1-1/2 tsp.	2 tsp.	2-1/2 tsp.
Vitamin & Mineral Supplement	Use according to directions on the label.					
Enzyme Supplement	Use according to directions on the label.					

When you serve the food, you can add additional nutrients as well as variety by mixing in a few extras from the list that follows.

Those who want to be scientific about a homemade diet and aren't afraid of some in-depth study can learn exactly which meats and grains are best for their dogs according to traditional Chinese medicine in the book *Four Paws, Five Directions,* by Cheryl Schwartz, D.V.M. This thorough book explains how certain meats and grains can be better depending on the dog's constitutional type. Without going into detail here, this simply means that a dog's diet can be tailored to help counteract imbalances in his physiology. The factors that are used to determine the best types of foods for your dog include whether she is sluggish, laid-back and calm, overweight, assertive, wanting attention, and so on.

The Extras: By adding some raw foods or high quality supplements, you will be upgrading the quality and adding energy and nutrients to the diet. This is especially important if you are feeding canned food or kibble (or a mixture of the two). ***At the very least, include some raw vegetables daily.*** Here are some of the raw foods Dr. Mary Brennan recommends:[6]

- *Raw vegetables:* Add 1/8 to 1/4 cup of raw vegetables for each 10 pounds of your dog's weight. Choose one of the following that your dog likes best: grated carrot, zucchini, chopped lettuce, green beans, or broccoli. (Or give a whole raw carrot as a treat from time to time.)

- *Raw fruits:* Give a small amount of raw fruit such as apples, grapes, and watermelon a couple times a week.

- *Organic meat:* Add 1/8 to 1/4 cup of broiled or baked organic meat for each 10 pounds of your dog's weight. Choose from chicken, turkey, beef, or lamb; free range is the best. Since most dogs already get plenty of protein in their diet, add this extra meat to the food only once or twice a week (or give as a treat).

- *Raw egg:* Feed a raw egg once a week or so. To minimize the possibility of salmonella poisoning, use fresh organic eggs from range-fed chickens.

- *Garlic:* Add 1/2 clove of minced fresh garlic to the food for each 10 pounds of your dog's weight or give a capsule of Kyolic or other highpotency garlic. If desired, garlic can be added daily.

- *Acidophilus:* Add 1/4 to 1/2 teaspoon acidophilus liquid or powder or the contents of one capsule *once a week.* Acidophilus is found in

---

[6] Brennan and Eckroate, pages 92–93.

the refrigerator section of natural foods stores. This will help the body keep a proper balance of beneficial bacteria.

🦴 *Yogurt:* Give 1/8 to 1/4 cup for a small dog or 1/2 to 3/4 cup for a large dog. Use a plain, natural culture yogurt from the health food store. Add to the food or serve as a treat occasionally, up to several times a week.

🦴 *Cottage cheese and goat's milk:* Cottage cheese is an excellent source of protein that is easy to digest. Add a small amount to the food up to three times a week. If your dog is ill, cottage cheese can be fed daily. Goat's milk is naturally homogenized and therefore easy to digest. It also has a more complete nutrient balance than cow's milk. Do not feed cow's milk, cream, or half-and-half; they often cause diarrhea since dogs don't have the proper enzymes to digest these products.

🦴 *Vitamin and mineral supplements:* Choose a vitamin and mineral supplement for dogs made from high quality natural ingredients by a natural pet products company. These products come in powders that are added to the food, such as Anitra's Vita-Mineral Mix (from Halo, Purely for Pets), Body Guard (from Pro-Tec), or Good Gravy (from Pet Nutrition). Other products, such as Vita-Dreams (from Halo, Purely for Pets), come in the form of tasty chewable supplements.

🦴 *Antioxidant supplements:* Antioxidants are supplements that combat the body's toxic invaders called free radicals. Beta-carotene and vitamins C and E are called antioxidant supplements because they play a supportive role in this process. In addition, there are products on the market made from whole food sources such as sprouted wheat that promote the body's own antioxidant enzyme supplies. These products include Bioguard and Vitality from Biogenetics. (Even dogs that have food sensitivities to wheat are generally able to take these supplements with no problem because the protein gluten found in the grain of wheat is not found in the wheat sprouts.)

Changing Your Dog's Diet

When you put your dog on a high quality diet, it's likely you will notice the difference in a few days or weeks. Ongoing health problems may disappear. The dog will have more energy, a shinier coat, less "dog odor," fewer bowel movements, and less gas.

However, it sometimes takes a few days or a week for a dog to adjust to a radical change in the diet. A high quality, *nutrient dense* diet can cause a temporary cleansing process. The most common short term symptoms of this adjustment are looser stools and more gas. You can minimize any upset to the dog's system by gradually incorporating the new diet over a ten-day period. Unless your dog has a sensitivity or allergy to one of the ingredients in the food, the transition to the higher quality diet will lead to a more youthful, energetic appearance in short order.

> *Note:* **If you think your dog is suffering from a food sensitivity or allergy, check with your veterinarian or use the muscle checking method of testing the food as described in The Natural Dog, by Mary Brennan.**

Ingredient Number 2: Play

> *Did you hear about the Border collie that went to see his veterinarian? The vet told him to stick out his tongue and go stand in front of the window. The dog followed the directions and then asked, "What's this for?" The vet said, "Nothing. I just don't like that springer spaniel in the house across the way."*

A bridge of communication between you and your dog is created and strengthened with the introduction of fun and humor, which are the very essence of play. Your dog will learn much more quickly if your attitude is playful. Certainly both your own as well as your dog's stress levels are reduced when you're having fun. A smile, a laugh, a good natured grin speak volumes. Just as humor can bring down communication barriers among people of different cultures, so too does it bridge the gap between species.

Humor is a release valve for the ever present stresses of everyday life. It isn't enough to say anger has no part of the training process. The idea is that fun, playfulness, and humor play a huge role. With the "ingredient" of play, you make the training process a game.

> *A Great Pyrenees falls out of a tenth-story window. He is lying there, surrounded by a crowd, when a police officer comes up and asks, "What happened?" The dog responds, "I don't know. I just got here myself."*

Patty Ruzzo, a well known dog trainer, has aptly stated that there is no such thing as obedience training—it's all about tricks. From the dog's point of view, that makes perfect sense. Sitting, lying down, coming when called—it's all about getting your dog to do things because it's in her best interest. This is easy when you make it fun. Playfulness is an attitude that benefits both you and your dog.

I suggest a minimum of two 15-minute periods of nonviolent play each day. If your dog initiates the play period, such as nudging you with a ball and asking you to throw it, this is a wonderful way to practice nonviolent dog training. Simply ask her to do something, like sit or lie down first, and then throw the ball as a reward.

> *A dog had a dream that God told her to get her act together. So, she joined a 12-step program, bought some new clothes, and started practicing yoga. She now had a healthy glow and looked like a new canine. Suddenly, she was struck by lightning and wound up in heaven, where God didn't talk to her. She shouted to God, "You told me in my dreams to better myself! I joined a 12-step program, got a new wardrobe, and took weekly yoga classes. Now you don't even talk to me!" God responded, "Don't holler at me. I didn't recognize you."*

Play affects the development of the physical, mental, and emotional life of your dog. Proper play helps to develop your dog's coordination, timing, and the skills needed for hunting and self-defense. You can provide all kinds of playful stimulation by enrolling in agility, flyball, herding, or water work classes. See more on this later in this chapter under Ingredient Number 5: Exercise.

Play also includes the use of toys. But toys should not be left around for the dog to play with by herself. If you provide the toys, your dog's attention is directed to you as the source of entertainment. If you're the source, your dog will more readily listen to what you have to say because she can access the toys only through you. You may, however, permit an exception to the rule and leave one or two chew toys around to relieve boredom.

Suggested Toys

Chew toys: Although there are lots of chew toys available for dogs today, a few of them are in a class by themselves. I suggest Nyla™ bones and natural, preservative- and dye-free rawhide bones to keep your dog's interest and massage the gums. They also tend to last awhile. Whatever you give your dog to chew on, *make sure you supervise.* The last thing you want a dog to do is choke on a small piece. I discourage chewies made from hooves and pig ears.

Smart toys: I also recommend so-called smart toys that you can fill with treats before you go to work, such as Kongs,™ Buster Cubes,™ and food-dispensing plastic balls. Dogs can have hours of fun playing with these toys and intermittently being rewarded when a treat falls out.

People toys: Soft Frisbees, tennis balls, and virtually anything else your dog might have fun with as long as it's nontoxic.

Squeaky toys: Squeaky toys are great but make sure you strictly supervise their use as many dogs love ripping them open to find the squeaker inside, which can be a choking hazard.

Bubbles: Some dogs love playing with bubbles. So buy some non-toxic bubbles and have a ball!

ILLUSTRATION 2

Suggested toys include smart toys such as Kongs, Buster Cubes, and other treat-dispensing toys, as well as soft Frisbees, Nyla bones, squeaky toys, and tennis balls. Natural, preservative-free rawhide bones are also acceptable, but only when you are able to supervise.

Before I forget, what vegetable do dogs like the most? *Collie-flower.*

So let the games begin. Start with hide-and-seek, which is described on page 168. And, by the way, be sure to tell your dog a joke every day, too. He may not comprehend the words, but he'll sure get the feeling!

Ingredient Number 3: Socialization

We ask our dogs to live with us under our terms and conditions. Therefore, it's important to socialize them so they can more easily adapt to their human family, neighbors, and other animals. Socialization deals with stimulating the five senses. It is the exposure to sights, sounds, smells, tastes, and touch. Socialization is interaction with life and all it has to offer, and being able to adapt to its challenges. "It's about surviving errors," as Dr. Karen Overall puts it.

If a dog is deprived of social stimulation, both physical and emotional health are compromised. It has been proven that the brain of an animal that is not exposed to a full range of life's sensory input is actually smaller than the brain of other animals. On the other hand, a wolf that lives in the wild and has a highly challenging range of sensory input from his natural environment has a brain that is up to one-sixth larger than the average domesticated dog of the same size and proportion. New research may explain some of the reasons for the difference in the size of the brain in animals that are exposed to sensory input and those that are not. Scientists have recently released the results of two different studies that show some kinds of physical and mental exercise promote the growth of new neurons, while also measurably prolonging the survival of existing brain cells. This means that the brain is revitalized, "spurring the growth of new brain cells responsible for learning and memory."[7]

Because of the lack of physical, emotional, and mental stimulation (socialization), many domesticated animals don't get along well with others. A lack of socialization also fosters other problems, including health problems, obsessive tail chasing, self-mutilation, scratching, biting, destruction of the environment (including walls, floors, and furniture), interminable spells of barking, chewing, and various manifestations of aggression. Although there can be other causes for these problems, poor socialization or a total lack of socialization is an important factor in most cases.

The first sixteen weeks of a dog's life are the most influential in shaping the adult dog's temperament and behavior. Conscientious breeders begin handling pups as soon as they're born to get them used to human touch and start the socialization process. All through puppyhood, the mother dog socializes her pups through her tactile stimulation, using her tongue to massage her puppies to teach them how to control their elimination. She talks to them in a language made up of sounds, touches, smells, and body postures. And as the pups grow older, the bond of social familiarity is strengthened through this network of communication. They become aware of brothers and sisters vying for their mother's milk and learn the language both nature and their mother patiently teach them.

The following will give you a general idea of what to look for in your dog's behavior during various stages of his maturation. These periods can vary somewhat depending on size and breed. And you'll

---

[7] Hotz, Robert Lee, "Active Mind, Body Linked to Brain Growth," *Los Angeles Times,* February 23, 1999, page A1.

also see some overlap between the periods. It's important to remember not to ask more of your dog than she can possibly do. Physically, mentally, emotionally, and socially, each dog has his or her own individual personality, ability, and unique way of doing things. The skill is learning when to challenge, when to back off, and how to balance the two.

Stages of Maturation

8 weeks to 10 weeks

This is called the critical imprint or fear impact period. It is during these two weeks that sharp noises and rough handling can have a dramatic impact on behavior. It can take months, and in some cases, years, to recover from experiences that frighten a puppy during this time period. It is important to continue socializing your dog during these two weeks. However, try to avoid taking him to places where he could be traumatized. Some behaviorists recommend not taking the puppy to the veterinarian during this time period. Please use common sense, however!

8 weeks to 16 weeks

This period overlaps with the previous one because it is from eight weeks to sixteen weeks that your puppy goes through what is called the primary socialization window. Studies have shown that it is during this period of time that socialization, or the lack of it, has the most impact on the shaping of your dog's temperament and behavior. It's very important that you continue to socialize and train your puppy during these formative weeks. This will help build your dog's self-confidence and really develop her emotional "bounce-back" ability. This means the more she interacts with her environment and is provided the opportunity to learn from her mistakes, the more even-tempered she will become. Training includes housetraining (see Eliminating, page 207) and beginning to work on behaviors such as sit, lie down, stand, stay, come when called, heel, go to your spot, etc. It's also very important that you teach your dog to control his biting during this period (see Mouthing, page 211). Even at this early age, puppies respond well to clicker and target training.

4 months to 8 months

Called the "first independence" window, the four- to eight-month period could be likened to the terrible twos in human maturation. It's a dog's job to "test" the social order in various contexts up to the point of emotional maturity, which happens between the ages of two and four. The dog "tests" by not coming when called, not listening when you ask him to do things, and generally being like a typical kid testing his limits. It is also during this period that the second set of teeth begin to appear. Make sure you provide plenty of proper chew toys to help avoid chewing and biting problems during this teething period. This period is also sometimes referred to as the "avoidance" period because puppies often become suspicious and hesitant about being introduced to new things. Keep your training routine fun and maintain socialization exercises but be sure to go at your dog's own learning pace.

6 months to 18 months

This is the "teenage period" in a dog's life, the period of sexual maturity. Your dog will continue to test you during this period, possibly a little more aggressively. Once again, there may be moments when she may suddenly seem reluctant to try something new. It is your job to be your dog's guardian—which means no matter what she does, you will maintain your loving, patient, and consistent direction. This is also the period during which neutering or spaying should be done. (If you are going to breed your dog, be sure you are in the position to take responsibility for every puppy.) Around the eleventh or twelfth month in particular, your dog may severely try your patience and act like a teenage bozo. Don't worry—it's just part of the growing up process. There will also be moments when he seems to be God's gift to dogs. In a few more months, he'll be back to being his happy, jovial, rambunctious self. The bottom line is be patient, be consistent, and continue your compassionate role as guardian and protector.

18 months to 4 years

During the early portion of this period, your dog's behavior may be marked by an increase in aggression and a renewed testing to see who's the boss. Sometimes two previously friendly dogs may suddenly seem to be at odds. In the later stage of this period, when your dog reaches social maturity, her behavior will level out and she'll recognize how she can get what she wants. In most cases I have found it takes about eighteen months for a dog to settle in to his environment and finally understand what's expected. With an optimum training environment you can get reliable behavior in less time. However, in the typical busy household in which training is inconsistent, and because of the dog's hormonal stages, it is only at eighteen months that your dog can be expected to reliably respond to your requests. There will still be ups and downs in behavioral reliability but if you maintain an even keel, you will find that, with consistent training, your dog really does get the picture of who she is as a member of the family and what is expected of her. Because of your dog's increasing reliability at this stage, this is a good time for her to be involved in animal-assisted therapy—visiting hospitals, nursing homes, and schools.

While, in most cases, the old adage "you can't teach an old dog new tricks" is simply not true, it does take longer and require more effort to modify an older dog's behavior if socialization has not been provided during the early development periods. Since smaller dogs mature more quickly than larger breeds, some dogs reach social maturity as early as eighteen months while others don't reach this stage until much later.

Socialization is an important part of your own bonding process with your dog. To understand this emotion-behavior link, it is helpful to look at a concept from the world of psychology called "social facilitation." If one dog is chewing a bone, the second dog will want to join in—normally by stealing the bone, even if he already has one. If one puppy goes to get a drink from a bowl, all the puppies decide to get a drink. If one dog starts digging, others seem to think, "What's so good over there? I better start digging with her." This is the way you get a dog interested in toys. Make a huge fuss over a new toy and watch your dog's interest grow.

Of course, social facilitation also occurs in other ways between humans and dogs. Dogs often pick up on our emotions and behaviors and follow suit. When I am called to do private consultations, I often find problems are directly related to people inadvertently teaching their dogs to be aggressive because of their own fears. In her book, *Excelerated Learning,* Dr. Pamela Reid says, "People socially transmit fears to their dogs via social facilitation all the time. Women who are wary of passing by men at night may quickly end up with a dog that barks ferociously at men. Some people have a hard time because of tentativeness or fear when someone is following behind. The dog, feeling the tension, quickly develops the same fear and, sometimes generalizes the fear to all strangers or all dogs. This sort of problem is extremely difficult to treat."[8] In short, there are many subtle ways in which we communicate our emotions to our dogs that directly affect their behavior. And, of course, many positive emotions are also transferred from human to dog.

Socialization feeds all of the senses and safely, positively promotes emotional growth, confidence, and security. There are two types of socialization—active and passive. You are involved in actively socializing your dog when you introduce her to toys, games, neighbors, friends, and strangers. With passive socialization, nature is involved to a greater degree. Dogs learn by interacting with the sights, sounds, smells, and touches of other animals, plants, and environments while away from you. They learn the consequences of their actions as individuals on their own. Obviously, it's important to provide an environment in which you avoid life-threatening situations, such as putting your dog in a room with a literal or figurative pack of wolves. But the more she can learn and experience about herself on her own, the more she develops confidence, learns to adapt, and is able to bounce back from stressful situations.

Your dog is socialized through playing, being groomed, training, and the everyday challenges you place before her. Take your dog everywhere—in your car and to the office, supermarket, park, dog

---

[8] Reid, Pamela J., Ph.D., *Excel-erated Learning*, James and Kenneth Publishers, 1996, page 167.

training classes, and visiting friends and relatives. Take her to the veterinarian's office for a visit even when she's not going for an appointment with the veterinarian. (However, wherever you take your dog, do not leave her unattended!)

Proper socialization contributes to fostering nonaggression. Poor socialization or the lack of socialization may create avoidance and fear of whatever or whomever the dog hasn't been exposed to. Here are some socialization exercises you can introduce to your dog:

🦴 *Handle your dog.* If your dog is a puppy, lift her in the air while gently stroking her and speaking to her. Begin this handling and verbal communication as soon as you bring the puppy into your home, ideally between the seventh and eighth week, and continue safe handling for very short periods several times a day. For older dogs, begin the process at the point your dog accepts your touch and gradually work toward the point where she allows you to lift her. If your dog is too big to lift, you can work toward the point of the ultimate snuggle, holding and touching all over her body. Gradually extend the snuggling time until your dog trusts you for as long as you hold her. (See Handling on page 144.)

🦴 *Do environment enrichment exercises.* As the puppy grows, let her explore safe surroundings, both inside and outside; put toys and novel stimuli on the living room floor and in the yard without you. These items can include balls of different sizes (baseballs, basketballs, beach balls), stuffed animals, and lawn tools. Introduce other animals, with strict supervision, of course. (Review the safety precautions in Chapter 9.) Join an agility, flyball, herding, tracking, or water work class.

🦴 *Take your puppy to puppy kindergarten classes.* Remember, the more you socialize your dog early on, the more you shape her temperament and establish a loving bond. Find a class where your puppy can romp and roll with others.

Ingredient Number 4: Quiet Time

Just as humans sometimes need a time out from the day's activities, dogs also need a place where they can go to get away from it all. Find a place where she can go and not be disturbed and then create a safe spot such as a large cotton rug or mat, a kennel, a place underneath the table, or a doggy bed. In Part II we've provided instructions to help your dog learn to absolutely *love* going to her spot.

If you have children, teach them to respect your dog's safe area. This is especially important over the holiday season if your house is packed with partying people.

Ingredient Number 5: Exercise

For optimum health, dogs require the same four types of exercise that humans need—aerobic exercises, strength exercises, stretching exercises, and balancing exercises. The most common aerobic exercise for dogs is running. Of course, aerobic exercise can easily be incorporated in play since a dog runs while chasing balls, Frisbees, and bubbles. Flyball and agility training are also great opportunities to run.

Strength exercises are easy to include in your dog's daily routine. They include running up a hill, running through snow or sand, and, of course, swimming. You can help to maintain your dog's muscle tone and strength by teaching him to carry items in a pack strapped to his back or by hitching him up to a cart or wagon and having him pull your child down the street. Obviously, this must be done with a great deal of discernment. Whereas a malamute can pull a child's sled, it wouldn't really benefit a Chihuahua to pull a sled—even if you had a miniature toy sled that would match his size. Physical capabilities, age, health, and the way in which you train your dog all influence his strength level and how the various strength exercises will benefit him.

Stretching exercises are extremely helpful in keeping your dog's ligaments, tendons, and muscles supple, flexible, and healthy. Anyone who lives with animals is aware of their natural inclination to stretch. Most people recognize the value of stretching before they begin to exercise in order to minimize the possibility of strains and muscle pulls. When you ask your dog to fit into your daily exercise routine, it's important to keep his own stretching needs in mind so he won't get hurt either. The best way to help your dog stretch is to give him a daily massage. It doesn't have to take long—five minutes of massage a day is extremely beneficial.

In addition to the obvious therapeutic benefits, massage is also a terrific way to bond with your dog. In his book *The Healing Touch,*

Michael Fox, D.V.M., says: "The tender loving touch is essential for well-being and for the normal growth and development of all socially dependent animals. It would seem that their nervous systems require such stimulation either from the gentle licks of their mothers' tongues or the strokes of a caring human hand. As a seedling cannot thrive without the light of the sun, so, too, do our animal kin suffer without the energy of love. And it is through touch especially, that this energy can be given and reciprocated."[9]

In addition, massaging your dog also benefits you. In her excellent book *Four Paws, Five Directions,* Cheryl Schwartz, D.V.M., relates: "It has been shown through projects developed and publicized by Dr. Leo Bustad, while Dean at Washington State University Veterinary School in the 1980s, that stroking and touching an animal can help lower a person's blood pressure, increase self-esteem and establish a feeling of well-being."[10]

Among the massage techniques Dr. Schwartz shares in her book is the following: "The type of massage stroke you may be most familiar with is the long stroke using the flat of the hand and finger tips. This is known as 'effleurage.' Long strokes are good for the abdomen and larger muscle groups along the neck and back. Most animals enjoy these strokes. The pressure should be regulated according to what the animal tells you. He will move away if it is too hard or closer if it is not hard enough.

"Another useful stroke is like a rubbing motion, called 'friction.' Use the tips of your fingers and apply pressure in a forward and backward motion, usually beginning slowly, about 1 per second, and gradually increasing to 2 per second. I usually recommend that this be done between the shoulder blades and over the rump area or along the midline of the chest between the front legs extending down toward the abdomen."[11]

For more information and additional massage techniques, I suggest both Dr. Fox's and Dr. Schwartz's books.

The final category of exercise, balancing exercises, includes, among other exercises, walking on planks and balance boards, balancing on teeter-totters, and swinging on porch swings. These exercises are won-

---

[9] Fox, Michael W., D.V.M., *The Healing Touch,* Newmarket Press, 1990, page 9.
[10] Schwartz, Cheryl, D.V.M., *Four Paws, Five Directions,* Celestial Arts Publishing, 1996, page 119.
[11] Ibid., pages 122–123.

derful confidence builders. For some dogs, you can add sitting up in the begging pose, walking on hind or front legs, and climbing ladders. However, use common sense here; there are limitations on the balancing exercises that can be done by puppies, older dogs, and larger dogs. The best way to teach your dog how to balance is to enroll in an agility class in your area, where the necessary equipment is provided.

A dog should have a minimum of two fifteen-minute exercise periods each day. You can combine this with the play period to make it fun and easy.

Ingredient Number 6: Employment

If you don't give your dog a job to do, she will become self-employed. Employment is one of the nine ingredients that deserves special attention since it focuses on a seldom discussed area of dog training. As I've mentioned, the lack of a proper balance of mental, physical, and emotional stimulation is one of the main reasons that people have problems with their dogs. Employment is important because it not only provides this stimulation but also promotes and develops a sense of self, purpose, and pride.

To help explain and illustrate the importance of dogs "working" for their living, I developed the concept of "canine currency." All animals are genetically encoded with the instinct to expend energy in order to survive. This comes in the form of the hunt for food, safety from predators, and safety from the elements. They even have to work to mate and certainly to provide for their offspring. In most cases, when we take dogs into our homes, they no longer have to work for anything. This creates a situation where the dog is unemployed. So, to fill the vacuum, she may herd the children or retrieve the neighbor's newspaper. She may guard her food and toys or protect the home from the mail carrier and even nice Aunt Minnie. An unemployed dog might express her boredom by exhibiting manifestations of stress such as chewing on the furniture or even herself, ripping up linoleum, and destroying houseplants.

When you institute the concept of canine currency, you *pay* your dog in response to appropriate behavior, which is looked at as his work or his job. A dog then works for the currency, which is represented by food, affection, play, and special privileges. Having to work for a living challenges dogs and engages them in life. It eliminates boredom and gives them purpose. Once you institute the rule that "Nothing in life is free," your dog will work for almost everything and be happy to do so. Jobs include retrieving toys, doing tricks, and playing games. My dog Molly can answer the phone and throw it in the wastebasket if it's a bill collector. She can run an agility course, retrieve a ball under water, guard my car (nonviolently, of course), and demonstrate twenty different tricks when we visit elementary schools as part of our Nonviolence Works animal-assisted therapy program. Not a bad job!

Ingredient Number 7: Rest

Where should your dog sleep? Dogs are social animals and they are healthiest when they are with their family. When humans domesticated dogs, we became their family. Therefore, the ideal location for your dog's bed is around the smells and sounds of a family member. If you desire, it's okay to permit your dog to sleep on your bed. However, allow the dog on your bed only with your permission. This is a great training opportunity. Before allowing your dog on the bed, ask him to sit or lie down. When he does it, invite him onto the bed as a reward. Sleeping in the bedroom really strengthens the human-animal bond. I can't say enough about the benefits this provides.

Dogs usually prefer a "den," which can be anything from a fancy dog bed to an old chest that is cut open and inverted so the dog has a place to hide. Dogs sleep for up to sixteen hours a day. Again, just as with humans, undisturbed quality sleep is of utmost importance. It's important to teach children not to awaken a sleeping dog. When a child sees a dog running and whining in his sleep, she sometimes wants to wake him because "he's having a nightmare." However, this behavior while sleeping is part of a dog's natural sleep state, referred to as rapid eye movement (REM) sleep, where dreams abound. As with humans, REM sleep is important because it is the part of the sleep cycle in which some of our stress is resolved. REM sleep comes before, as well as between, the stages of sleep referred to as the dreamless states. The body enters its deepest relaxation during the dreamless states. Both the REM stage and the dreamless states of the sleep cycle are important for health. In short, let sleeping dogs lie.

Ingredient Number 8: Training

Since most of the rest of this book is about training, I'll say just a few words on the subject here. Training is also called puppy or dog etiquette. It helps a dog's maturity and self-confidence if you set the limits of behavior. In nonviolent, reward-based dog training, there is no jerking, hitting, kicking, shocking, shaking, ear pinching, or any other potentially harmful technique.

In reward-based training you control everything your dog wants. You control the food, freedom to go places, affection, toys, playtime, and access to the world. You provide comfort, safety, protection from weather, and health care. House rules simply state, "I will give you the world but you have to do something for me first." You will be playful, understanding, positive, and compassionate—but flexibly non-negotiable. Your dog will learn whatever behaviors you request and you will go at your dog's own learning speed; in essence, it'll take as long as it takes to get those behaviors. Several small sessions of three to five minutes each are better than two long sessions. I suggest two sessions in the morning and two or three in the evening. Many people find a great time to do training sessions is during commercials while they're watching television.

Dogs learn much faster when you create an environment where they build on their own success. You create a situation to reward behaviors you want, such as sitting, lying down, being quiet, or chewing on appropriate toys. If you reward what you want and use management to prevent your dog from repeating behaviors you don't want, training becomes a snap. Remember the rule: "Any behavior that is rewarded increases the probability that the dog will repeat that behavior."

Ingredient Number 9: Health Care

Health care needs vary with age, size, breed, and genetic influences, so check with your veterinarian for specific recommendations on the care of your dog. Proper grooming is an important part of your dog's health care regimen. The dog's coat, skin, nails, and ears should be cared for on a weekly basis at a minimum. Some veterinarians actually recommend brushing your dog's teeth on a daily basis, if possible. It is helpful if more than one member of the family learns to take care of the family dog since the time spent on these needs is a wonderful opportunity for socialization and bonding.

Since Western medicine is generally more invasive than alternative healing modalities and often utilizes pharmaceutical drugs that cause negative side effects, I prefer a veterinarian who includes holistic health care in his or her practice. Many times health problems can be more gently corrected through acupuncture, homeopathy, chiropractic, herbal medicine, and so on. I suggest you check with the holistic veterinary organizations listed in Appendix B for a list of holistic veterinarians in your area. You might also inquire at your local natural foods store, yoga school, or holistic medical doctor.

I also suggest that you read more on health care for your dog in *The Natural Dog: A Complete Guide for Caring Owners,* by Mary Brennan, D.V.M., and Norma Eckroate; *Dr. Pitcairn's Complete Guide to Natural Health for Dogs and Cats,* by Richard H. Pitcairn, D.V.M., Ph.D., and Susan Hubble Pitcairn; and *Four Paws, Five Directions,* by Cheryl Schwartz, D.V.M.

Combining the 9 Ingredients

As I've mentioned several times, you will often be able to fulfill more than one of the nine ingredients at a time, thereby making the whole process more interesting and keeping spirits high. The ideal way to provide almost all of the nine ingredients in a fun, simple way is to enroll in training classes. (See Appendix B for organizations that offer these classes.) I especially recommend agility, flyball, herding, water work, and tracking classes. In these programs, your dog is provided food (treats), play, training, socialization, exercise, and employment in one package. Then, when you get home she rests and has quiet time. Voilà! It's all there. On those days you're not in class, you can go to safe dog parks and throw Frisbees and balls, teach tricks, and play hide-and-seek.

To round it all off, you might want to pursue volunteer work in animal-assisted therapy. You and your dog can visit nursing homes and hospitals or present free programs on animal care in elementary schools. You might also want to volunteer at a local shelter to help the dogs that need help the most. These are all great opportunities to provide almost all of the nine ingredients for both you and your dog.

Suggested Daily Routine

Establishing a daily routine is very helpful in developing your puppy's or your new dog's sense of security and confidence. And it's also great for housetraining! Here is a sample of a daily routine you might try with your dog. It's just an idea of how Sparky's day might go. Obviously everyone's schedule is different and many variables exist. If you have a problem, contact a professional dog trainer who uses nonviolent training methods.

7–9 A.M.   *Take Sparky to eliminate and then feed him.*
First, wait for Sparky to sit and/or lie down before letting him out of his kennel or out of the bedroom. Begin by asking for one second of the sit or lie down and gradually extend the time. The reward is the freedom to go with you. Say "okay" to give your permission.

As Sparky eliminates, encourage and praise him with a word associated with this behavior, like "outside" or "hurry-up." Make one place the area for elimination. To encourage him to eliminate quickly and in the place you specify, when he finishes you might give him a great treat like a small piece of turkey. Bring him inside and let him investigate and say hello to people, but be sure that everyone waits for him to sit before petting him. Unless he's getting into mischief, ignore him until he does what he's asked. Play the magnet game with him. (See page 159.)

Then take him for a walk. Practice heeling, coming when called, sitting, and walking without pulling.

When you return home and bring him in the house, do not immediately put him in his kennel or other safe area and leave for the day. Let him explore, or play with him for a little while, or give him a wonderful toy to chew on or play with so he doesn't associate coming into the house with something negative. I suggest a Nyla bone, a "carrot" bone, a Kong, or a Buster Cube.

When you feed Sparky, practice come, sit, and/or down before putting the dish down.

If Sparky is still a puppy (up to one year old) take him outside within a few minutes after eating to eliminate again.

9 A.M.–noon *Allow Sparky to rest.*

noon–1 P.M. *If Sparky is a puppy, take him outside to eliminate again.*
After Sparky eliminates, encourage and praise him as mentioned before. Make it fun! Vary the routines and vary your rewards. Throw toys and play hide-and-seek and "find it." Do not chase him; have him chase you. If possible, let him play with a *safe* neighborhood dog.

1–5 P.M. *Allow Sparky to rest.*

5–10 P.M. *Take Sparky outside to eliminate and take a walk, then give him dinner.*
Repeat above activities and games. Give Sparky his dinner. While on your walk, let him interact with as many sights, sounds, and smells as is safe. When interacting with other people, tell them he's in training and ask them to follow "approach and greet" protocols. (See Dog Etiquette—How to Greet a Dog on page 77.) Praise his good behaviors. Be patient. When you return home, give him supervised free time in the house. If he becomes too excited, tether him in a social area and play the magnet game with him. (Never tether a dog unsupervised!) Play with his favorite toys with him. Massage him. This is also a good time to join a dog training class or agility, herding, or flyball class. Other nights you can read some good dog books or watch a training video together!

10 P.M. *Take Sparky outside to eliminate and for a final walk.*
Go on a final walk and then tuck Sparky in for the night.

(Post on refrigerator)

Daily Routine for _____

Establishing a daily routine is very helpful in developing your puppy's or new dog's sense of security and confidence (and it's great for house-training!). In the spaces below, list the times set aside for feeding, play, socializing, grooming, exercising, and training, as well as the family member whose responsibility it is for that day and time. Remember, if you don't know what you want your dog to do, your dog can't figure it out either. It's best to formulate your specific behavioral goals and create an environment and schedule where your dog can build on success rather than having to correct your dog.

7 A.M.–9 A.M.

9 A.M.–noon

noon–1 P.M.

1 P.M.–5 P.M.

5 P.M.–10 P.M.

10 P.M.

Praise, Praise, Praise all appropriate behavior. Ignore your dog's inappropriate behavior unless it is harmful to him, you, or the environment.

chapter three

Stress and Your Dog's Behavior

Many years ago, at a large zoo, primates were getting sick and dying. After much study, stress management experts decided the monkeys' immune systems were being compromised due to a lack of stress. They weren't getting enough physical, mental, and emotional stimulation. In short, their lives were just too routine and dull. So the zookeepers constructed a life-size, lifelike predator in the form of a mechanical lion. On a random schedule, the lion would appear out of the bushes, growling away. The monkeys would run screeching to the safety of their trees. This simulated threat improved the health and longevity of the monkeys by stimulating them, thereby strengthening their immune systems. Because they were always successful in escaping from the "predator," these incidents proved to be a positive stress.

All of us, dogs and humans alike, need stress in our lives. We need to be challenged in order to stay healthy and evolve. We need to face challenges and successfully adapt to these challenges— physically, emotionally, and mentally. Studies have shown how animals raised without the stress of physical and emotional stimulation—stress that challenges but doesn't overwhelm—actually have less gray matter in their brains. This means their health and growth is actually impaired by a lack of stress.

For both dogs and humans, all stress—both positive and negative—is defined as the body's reaction to change in the environment or a perceived change in the environment. These changes include such everyday occurrences as being late for work, meeting a job deadline, paying bills, or making dinner by the time the family gets home. Of course, external stressors also include bigger events in a person's life, including job changes, such as being hired, promoted, or fired; getting married or divorced; moving; having a baby; illness; or exposure to extreme heat or cold.

Your body also reacts to changes in your *internal* environment. Stressors that impact you internally include emotions such as anger, worry, or anything that you perceive as a threat, real or imagined. This is an important point—it is how we perceive the world that affects us. If we can change how we feel about events in our lives, they will have less negative impact on our health and well-being.

What Is Stress Anyway?

Balancing your checkbook might not cause you any stress at all; however, if you have trouble with bookkeeping or believe your checking account balance might be overdrawn, it might be a big stress. Stress is very individual—some people thrive on situations that other people perceive as overwhelming.

Any stressful event can trigger a survival instinct that has been part of our genetic code since caveman days. Referred to as the "fight or flight" response, this survival instinct tells us we have two choices: to fight our adversary or to take flight. Even though we rarely find ourselves in the life-or-death situations of our ancient ancestors, the nervous system reacts to any stressful situation with this instinctive response. Let's say a deadline is approaching. The heart begins to pound, the blood pressure spikes, the pulse races, and the amount of perspiration increases. The body releases adrenaline, which causes the digestive system to shut down, and steroids such as cortisol surge into the bloodstream to pump up the energy level and add to muscle strength. At the same time, blood flow is directed to the muscles and the pupils dilate. Stress can also cause us to unconsciously change our breathing rate from longer breaths to very short, shallow breaths. When this happens the volume of air we inhale is greatly reduced.

The fight or flight response kicks in whenever you are feeling threatened. But, as with some of the examples I mentioned earlier, the threat doesn't have to be extreme. If you are startled every time your boss calls your name or every time your dog starts to bark, your body automatically goes through this reaction. If the stress continues over a period of time, you maintain a level of tension throughout most or all of the day and can actually forget how to relax. After a while you go from what's called the resistance stage, where the body is able to handle the stress of everyday living and stay healthy, to the exhaustion stage, where your body just can't take it anymore. This is where illness and injury occur.

Stress Thresholds

When there are too many stressing stimuli presented all at once or, to put it another way, when too much stress accumulates, the stress threshold is compromised. In other words, there's just too much on the plate to deal with. Accumulated stress must be expressed in some way or you or your dog will become susceptible to illness and accidents. Think of it this way: Let's say you take your dog to the veterinarian. Upon returning home, a friend comes over to visit, along with her not-too-friendly Akita. Now the kids come home from school and one of them accidentally steps on your dog's foot. Someone turns the television on at a high volume and, at the same time, the Akita eyes your dog's bone. Then the doorbell rings and a guy in a uniform enters with a package. Get the picture? Overload for both you and your dog. Normally your dog is fine. But like building blocks being piled one on top of another, the stress accumulates and rises above the dog's stress management threshold. The dog needs to vent. If he doesn't, it's possible for an overload of stress to lead to acts of aggression. With some dogs, biting is the natural response.

One of the greatest stresses is not being able to predict the future. This means we feel hopeless or powerless over our own lives. Think of what it's like to be a dog. Dogs are geared for routines. So what happens if routine is missing from a dog's life? Imagine not knowing when and where your next meal is coming from, or not being able to go where you want, or wondering if another animal is just around the corner waiting to attack you. If an animal is continually in a state of "I don't know what's going to happen next," the stress can become unbearable. Getting to know your dog and his stress threshold is the first step in establishing a healthy environment. The second step is knowing what to do about it. Among other things, that's what this book is all about.

Stress *management* is the ability to cope with stress by minimizing its causes and/or by raising an individual's stress threshold. Each dog is an individual with his own unique ability to handle stress. However, a dog doesn't have the ability to consciously choose to handle stress overload. His stress threshold can be raised, however, with your help. For example, a dog's reaction to a child stepping accidentally on his foot might be to bite the child. Through systematic desensitization, however, that same dog can learn to respond to the same situation by jumping up and looking for a treat.

Desensitization means getting the dog used to the threatening event gradually by increasing the stress over a period of time, until she perceives the formerly stressful event as no big deal or even as something positive. Many species have been trained to accept experiences that are painful. Some animals are even taught to help facilitate the event that causes the pain. Baboons learn to put their arms out so veterinarians can stick a needle in and do blood tests. Killer whales slide out of the water and lift a fin for the same purpose. And elephants are taught to lift their massive feet through a fence so caregivers can file their nails. The training that is required to shape these behaviors takes time and requires an environment where an animal can build on success. The nine ingredients in Chapter 2 are the means to create a healthy environment to do just that.

Four Ways Dogs Manifest Stress

Dogs basically express or manifest stress in four ways: oral, vocal, somatic, and/or visceral. These manifestations of stress can include behaviors such as chewing on furniture, clothing, or people (oral); barking, whimpering, and whining (vocal); scratching, running around, pawing, or jumping (somatic); or eliminating or vomiting (visceral). All of these manifestations are basically nervous energy being released. In human terms, these behaviors are similar to our little expressions of stress such as unconsciously biting the nails, speaking too fast or too loudly, or squirming or fidgeting.

Many of these manifestations of stress have certain meanings to other dogs and are also used as language. Turid Rugaas, a Norwegian behaviorist, labeled some of these behaviors as "calming signals." In psychology circles, they are called "displacement behaviors." Among the signals Rugaas labels as "calming" are blinking the eyes, looking away, sniffing the ground, turning to the side, licking the lips, and yawning. Watch your dog closely so you will learn to recognize what she is "thinking" and what she is "saying." All of these signals are recognizable to humans if we watch for them. Your dog may be reaching her stress threshold if she starts panting and drooling, or shivering, or if her paws become sweaty. When a dog reaches the threshold of distress, learning stops. Once you learn to recognize your dog's stress threshold, you have entered into a new level of fluency in canine communication and life with Fido will be much more pleasant. (I'll cover more about canine communication in Chapter 5.)

When a Person's Stress Leads to Abusive Situations

Of course, just as with dogs, distress is debilitating to us humans, too. It negatively impacts both our physical and emotional health when we internalize our stress and bottle it up. This bottled-up stress can result in headaches, ulcers, and other serious health problems or even alcohol or drug abuse. It becomes an even greater problem when it leads to hostility and manifests as physical or emotional abuse toward others. When a person's stress is directed toward a dog, he might be assuaging his own pent-up emotions, but in the process the dog is learning something the person probably doesn't want to teach. For example, let's look at a classic example of stress when it is displaced or redirected as aggression. We'll call it the scenario of "the old man has a bad day at the office and comes home and kicks the dog." It goes something like this:

1. The man walks in and the dog recognizes the visual, sound, and scent cues of the person by immediately associating his body language with past experiences. These physical cues include the

person's shallow and restricted breathing, muscle tension, and the scent of stress hormones being given off.

2. The dog remembers that the person yells, hits, or does something else negative when he acts, sounds, and smells this way. The dog responds submissively by putting his tail between his legs, putting his ears back, crouching, rolling over, and licking his lips. Just as a person might act submissively in a threatening situation by cowering, shaking, or running away, the dog's behavior is a signal that he is doing everything he knows to do to tell the person that he "submits." In human terms, the dog's response says, "Okay, I surrender. You don't have to escalate the behavior and you don't have to hurt me."

3. Oblivious to what the dog is communicating, the person continues to fume about what happened at work during the day, slamming doors, yelling, and throwing the mail on the table.

4. Because the person continues to use the same body language, the dog sees that his submissive behavior just isn't enough and feels he must submit even more. He then urinates on the Persian rug, saying, in essence, "See, I defer to you even more."

5. The person now puts his attention on the dog urinating on the carpet and redirects his still unresolved anger. He yells, threatens, picks the dog up by the nape of the neck and shakes him, and then throws him out the door.

6. Now the dog really begins to have problems. He has done everything he could to communicate but nothing worked.

In this situation, the dog has learned nothing about what *not* to do, is thoroughly confused as to what he's *supposed* to do, and begins manifesting more behaviors that will get him in trouble, such as chewing, digging, escaping from the yard, or even biting. This is normally the point where I'm called in for a behavioral consultation. That's if the dog is lucky and hasn't been taken to be euthanized. In the next chapter, I'll share some additional tools so you can implement a stress management routine for the sake of your dog as well as yourself.

chapter four

The Human Emotion and Dog Behavior Link: The Bridge of Breath

A few years ago I conducted an informal study, asking about thirty professional dog trainers what percentage of the dog's behavior is influenced by a person's emotions. Those I surveyed felt that 75 percent of a dog's behavior is related to the emotional state of his handler. It wasn't a scientific study but the results were pretty clear. These experts agree that how we feel has a major impact on how our dogs behave. In turn, our feelings influence what we do, what we say, and how we say it.

Most people have experienced this emotion-behavior connection with their dogs. When we're upset, our dogs get upset. When we're happy, they tend to be happy. When we're frightened, our dogs may feel threatened. Dogs learn to associate our behaviors with certain consequences, and the cycle starts with our emotions. From feelings of joy and happiness to frustration, despair, anger, and rage, our emotions are translated into physical expressions. Dogs are able to "read" even the most subtle of these human behaviors through our body language, smells, and breathing patterns.

When people bring their dogs to my classes for the first time many of them are pretty tense. The dogs, pretty excited themselves, feed off people's stress. They jump, bark, and pull them all over the place. As a result, the people get more anxious—and some of them get angry and frustrated. They mutter "I'm sorry. He's not this way at home," or "Fido, knock it off!" followed by a pop on the leash. Animal behaviorists and trainers, such as those who work with dolphins and killer whales, are well aware of how much their own stress affects their training ability. To minimize the degree to which a person's feelings can impact a training session, they establish precise training schedules in strictly controlled environments.

On the plus side, the strong emotional connection between ourselves and our dogs can also be used to benefit both of us. So let's explore ways to optimize this emotional link.

The Benefits of Complete Breathing

Twenty-five years ago I decided to explore alternative therapies to get a grip on my health problems. As a child I missed 25 percent of my grade school classes because of asthma. I had a severe allergy to nuts and thirty-seven other allergies ranging from grass to pollen to dust. I was a mess. The fact that I began smoking cigarettes as a teenager while using an inhaler for my asthma also, of course, spoke of a certain lack of common sense. It must have been the lack of oxygen.

Actually, before resorting to alternative therapies, I visited a major hospital to see if my problem could be handled once and for all. But the news was not good. I was told frankly that I would have to continue on my medications and inhaler and learn to live with these health problems for the rest of my life. That idea was unacceptable. I was finally motivated to search for alternative therapies, which led me to the practice of yoga. After six months of practice, I no longer needed to use an inhaler and my desire for cigarettes disappeared. Within two years, my lifelong allergies had diminished to a short list of five. Now I'm down to only three.

As a person who was close to death a number of times due to my inability to breathe, I cannot express strongly enough what breathing exercises can do. As a student and practitioner of yoga, I know that breathing exercises can lead to a new level of peace, self-control, uncommon awareness, and power. Over the years I've become a little cynical and a real "prove it to me" kind of guy. I experiment, but until the experiment is true for me, I'm pretty nuts and bolts about the way

I view things. To me, faith is based on experience. With that in mind, let me share what my first yoga instructor told me years ago: "Try my suggestions for a few months. If these methods work for you, continue to practice them. If you see a direct influence, continue to practice them. If they don't work for you, throw them in the lake and try something else." I say the same thing here. Try the suggestions I list in this chapter. If they don't work for you and your dog, try something else.

It was only when I gave up smoking that I realized how much I had used cigarettes to handle my stress. Whenever I had a problem, out a cigarette would come. Smoking helped me to focus and concentrate and develop strategy. It was great. The tactile sensation, the fire, the oral fixation, and, of course, the nicotine were all part of why smoking was so addictive. The other appeal of smoking, of course, was how cool I looked in a James Dean kind of way. Of course, there was also a big downside—the health risks, sleeplessness, difficulty in breathing, smelling like an ashtray, and all the rest.

Among the many benefits of complete breathing are that more oxygen gets to the brain, the sympathetic and parasympathetic branches of the autonomic nervous system are balanced, and hormones such as endorphins, which increase your sense of well-being, are released. Now here's where the dog's amazing sense of smell comes into the equation. A dog's sense of smell is connected to the amygdala gland in the brain, which processes emotional behavior, and hence, influences physical behavior. Dogs can smell hormones released by a person's body. Through past positive associations, which are learned behaviors, a dog can actually gain an increased sense of well-being simply by smelling a person's hormones. This is a simplistic explanation of a complex process, but the bottom line is that your breathing and all it entails not only benefits you but also your wonderful canine partner via your relaxed body language and your smell.

The complete breath exercise (which I'll share later in this chapter) helps to reduce stress and tension while it gives an increased ability to focus and concentrate. When you do the complete breath, you'll actually have greater control of situations as they occur while, at the same time, you'll find that your creativity and intuition are increased. A round of three complete breaths takes only a minute to do and is a great way to begin every training session with your dog. I do this exercise every time I begin a training session and I teach it at the beginning of every class. I find it does wonders to put people in a relaxed frame of mind and instill a feeling of control.

People attending my classes may have wondered what a breathing exercise had to do with dog training, but to this day no one has ever questioned it. Perhaps that's because the benefits are so obvious after you do it the first time.

Finding Your Power Through Breath

Why is it that one person can be totally inspiring when giving a speech while another person might give the exact same speech and bore you to tears? Or why can one member of the family tell the dog to sit and get an immediate response from her, while the same dog totally ignores another member of the family every time he says sit? In part, it's because of the dog's training and reinforcement history. Clearly, the dog responds to the member of the family who worked more with her and rewarded her for sitting. But another, more subtle, difference has to do with the person's words and actions being infused with power. Dogs are more responsive to people whose will power is strong.

Dogs react not only to the gross manifestations of your body language, but also to the subtler energy manifestations of your will. When you start each training session with the complete breath exercise, you will find that it is easier to attract your dog's attention and that you are able to keep it longer. Dogs respond to the finer signals of your "mind-stuff" or thoughts. It's as if you've created a powerful magnetic attraction that draws your dog's attention. You've infused your words and actions with power. Really great animal trainers have developed this ability. Watch what happens when a skilled trainer walks into a roomful of dogs.

To understand how your will power can be heightened by a simple breathing exercise, it might be helpful to look at the Eastern view of what breath is and how it affects us. Breath actually carries with it a subtle but powerful energy. In yoga this energy in the breath is called "*prana*" and all the different breathing exercises are called "*pranayamas*." Other philosophies call this same energy "*chi*" or "*qi*," while Luke Skywalker knew it as "The Force."

Think of it this way: which light is more powerful—a streetlamp or a laser? The light that radiates from a streetlamp is diffused; it lights an entire area of the street. But when light is focused in a small direct beam as a laser, it is much more powerful. It can even burn through steel. In this same way, controlled breathing takes your own diffused energy and focuses it, making it laserlike.

When you focus on your breath, your concentration and your awareness of what's going on both externally and internally are increased. Your will power is no longer diffused by a myriad of distractions, so, in the process, it is also strengthened exponentially. You can then focus and concentrate on a singular thought or image and give it shape and power.

When training a dog, focus your energy and your concentration on the image of the behavior you want your dog to do. Your now-focused concentration and enhanced awareness will enable you to observe your dog in much greater detail. Eventually you will be able to actually "read" your dog and anticipate his behavior. As a result, you become more confident and relaxed, more aware, more alert, and more focused. Imagine how all this is going to affect your dog.

In addition to enhancing your will power, the state of relaxation that comes from complete breathing and visualization also puts you in the frame of mind to *respond* to your dog rather than having a knee-jerk *reaction*. As discussed in Chapter 1, this ability to respond rather than react opens you up so you can use your wisdom, creativity, intuition, and positive emotions. In short, it puts you in control of the situation.

Dogs are pure in their connection to nature—and nature is, after all, one big communication network. The breathing methods presented in this chapter will help reconnect you to that which you have known all along but may have forgotten—how nature communicates. And, there are added benefits—breathing exercises improve your overall health and studies show they also help relieve specific tension-related ailments such as headaches, chronic fatigue, asthma, and allergies. It's such a deal!

The Nuts and Bolts of Breathing

You've been breathing all of your life. But, if you're like many people, your breathing is shallow and, on occasion, you might even unconsciously hold your breath. The main goal of controlled breathing is to fully oxygenate your body. You need those oxygen molecules to travel down to the millions of tiny air sacs in the lung tissues. Once there, the oxygen passes through the membranes of the lungs and blood vessels to be picked up by the red blood cells. And at the same time—here's the important part—toxins and carbon dioxide are released through the lungs and oxygen is transported to the brain. This is why the complete breath makes you more relaxed while, at the same time, you become more alert and aware.

One of the reasons so many people have a shallow breathing pattern is that they breathe *exactly opposite* from the way that would give them the most oxygen. When asked to sit up straight and take a deep breath, most people do two things wrong. As they inhale, they puff up the chest like a frog and then draw the abdomen inward. Then, as they exhale, they slouch forward slightly as the belly area expands. Before reading further, take a deep breath and see if this is what you're doing. What moves first—your stomach or your chest?

If you're puffing up your chest, the air tends to fill only the upper part of your lungs. The small amount of air that is circulated to the lower portions of the lungs gets there through the force of gravity more than anything else. As a result, a lot of fresh, oxygen-rich air doesn't fully reach the bloodstream. This lack of oxygen affects everything you do.

With the complete breath you fill the lower portion of your lungs with air *first*, allowing your abdomen to expand, before moving the chest area. This allows your lungs to be completely filled with air, like filling a glass with water from bottom to top. Then, when you exhale, allow the lungs to slowly deflate until they are totally empty. It is not difficult to train yourself to breathe like this all the time. All it takes is practice, which will then retrain the muscles, and eventually this deep complete breathing will become natural. (Later in this chapter, I'll take you step-by-step through a complete breath exercise.)

The normal breath rate for both humans and dogs is between 10 and 30 times a minute. Many things, including the physical and emotional stimulation of a dog training class, affect this breath rate. For example, when humans and dogs pant due to excitement, fever, exercise, or heat, the faster breathing creates hypoxia, in which the tissues of the body become deficient in oxygen. And when you're tense, you just naturally take breaths that are more shallow. As a result, the reduced oxygen uptake further restricts the amount of oxygen going into the bloodstream and to your brain. This lack of oxygen also restricts your mental, physical, emotional, and intuitive processes because oxygen is the most accessible and health-giving source of energy you have.

The whole process looks like this: First, we get tense and restrict our breathing. Then our restricted breathing limits the amount of oxygen feeding our body. This then makes us more susceptible to diseases—and round and round we go. It's a vicious cycle.

Breath to the Rescue

Breathing exercises can increase your physical, mental, and emotional health and awareness and, at the same time, elicit different behaviors from your dog. For example, the complete breath exercise helps an energetic or stressed dog relax (see instructions on page 65). On the other hand, if your dog is lethargic and you want him to be more active, a few rounds of a panting breath will get his attention. A panting breath is easy to do: quickly repeat "ha, ha, ha, ha, ha" as you do when laughing. (However, when doing the panting breath, be sure you don't blow air directly into a dog's face. Some dogs may perceive that action as a threat; therefore, children should never do this exercise.)

Breathing can actually be used as an "occasion setter." That is, you can turn your dog's "action switch" on through the use of a breathing pattern. Just like picking up a leash means going for a walk or opening the bag of dog food means food is on the way, breathing can signal, "It's time to work" or "It's time to relax." The added benefit of using your breathing as an action switch is that you are also triggering your own physical, emotional, and mental power stations. You become more focused, your will power is "lasered," and, as a result, your dog responds to your requests that much quicker.

If you want to see an example of the impact of the complete breath on dogs, walk into a shelter full of barking dogs and do a series of deep breathing exercises. In a short time, most of the dogs will calm down demonstrably. If several people walk in and do this breathing at the same time, the results will be that much more dramatic.

Total Relaxation Exercise

Before doing the complete breath exercise (which follows), it is helpful to do this relaxation exercise. It's difficult to focus on relaxed breathing if the body isn't relaxed, so the first step in learning any breathing exercise is muscle relaxation. This takes a few minutes to read but it only takes a minute or two to actually do it. However, *don't rush.*

Practice in a place free from distractions, including your dog and, if necessary, turn the ringer on your phone off and put a "do not disturb" sign on your door. Also, adjust the heat and lighting so you will be comfortable. That way, your mental and physical muscles won't be startled or distracted by a phone ringing, an unpleasant light, extreme heat or cold, or other intrusions, such as a slobbery canine tongue.

1. Sit comfortably on a chair, on the floor, or on a pillow, keeping your back straight. If it's more comfortable for you, lean against the back of the chair or wall.
2. You might find it helpful to close your eyes. Gently take a deep breath.
3. Now inhale for three seconds, tense your entire body, including your face, hold it for three seconds, and then relax completely while exhaling for three seconds. Let your body go limp.

ILLUSTRATION 3

In Step 3 of the total relaxation exercise, tense your whole body, beginning by "making a fist" with your face and hands.

4. Now, for deeper relaxation, imagine your facial muscles softening and let any remaining tension drain out.

5. Slowly move your awareness down your body and relax the muscles in groups, starting with your face and going all the way down to your feet. Go through a mental checklist. ("Okay. Hmm—there's my left bicep. Relax. Relax. There's my left hand. "Go limp hand, relax." *And so on.*) Observe and relax, if possible, every muscle except those helping your body to sit up straight. They'll take care of themselves. Be sure to go through your entire body, including your feet and even the lines on the bottom of your feet!

6. Now move your awareness slowly back up your body in the opposite direction, from feet to head, checking for any remaining tension—and let it go. You can let it drain into the floor or imagine it's just evaporating—whatever works for you. Once you've mentally returned to your face and find it relaxed, you're ready for the complete breath exercise.

Complete Breath Exercise

This is one of the easiest and most effective breathing exercises. It can be practiced anywhere at any time. The complete breath consists of smoothly inhaling and exhaling through the nose for equal amounts of time. (It is also called the relaxation breath or diaphragmatic breathing.) The benefits of this exercise include greater relaxation, increased ability to focus, and improved concentration. It also helps you to become more acutely aware of the present moment—something dogs are naturally attuned to.

If you feel lightheaded or dizzy at any time, STOP! Take a break and try later. Then do just one complete breath instead of a series of three breaths.

ILLUSTRATION 4

Use the complete breath exercise to take a refreshing relaxation breath at any time, not just before training sessions.

1. This exercise can be done with your eyes closed or open. If you're at home, close your eyes. If you are driving a car or walking across a street while doing the exercise, keep them open.

2. Picture your lungs divided into three sections: top, middle, and lower. Begin to breathe in through your nose. (Be sure your mouth is closed so you are breathing through the nose only.) Allow the breath to fill the lower part of the lungs first, like water filling up a glass. As you inhale, allow your stomach to push out slightly. (If you tighten the stomach muscles inward, as most people do when breathing, it may take a few practice breaths to reverse this process.) When your lower lungs are full, imagine the oxygen filling the middle part of the chest. Then fill the top portion of your lungs. Your chest will expand and your shoulders will draw upward and back a little as you fill the top portion of your lungs.

3. *Without stopping when your lungs are full,* begin to exhale smoothly, again through your nose. Imagine that your lungs are two balloons that are slowly deflating. Near the end of the exhalation, expel any remaining breath by gently pushing your stomach muscles inward and a little upward toward the spine.

4. Immediately after the exhalation, gently begin to inhale your next breath.

At first, do a series of three complete breaths, timing your inhalation and exhalation so they are equal in length. Most people start with a count of three or four seconds for the inhalation and three or four seconds for the exhalation. Remember, the goal is to move smoothly from the exhalation into the inhalation of the next breath. Think of this transition as driving around gentle curves rather than sharp turns in the road. Slowly and smoothly work up to three breaths.

Over a few weeks' time, gradually extend the time of each inhalation and exhalation up to ten seconds. Don't hold the breath in between the inhalations and exhalations. Don't strain—let the length of each breath increase naturally. While you're beginning with a round of three breaths, your eventual goal is to extend the length of time you spend doing the exercise as well as the length of inhalations and exhalations. Spend one or two periods of five to ten minutes doing this relaxed complete breathing each day.

Another hint to help you concentrate and relax while doing the complete breath is to wear earplugs and listen to the sound of your breath. You'll be able to hear yourself breathe and be able to relax even more.

It's usually best to do these five- to ten-minute sessions before beginning your day or at the end of the day. In addition, however, for practical, everyday purposes, practice taking a series of three complete breaths several times throughout each day—before a training session with your dog, before the kids get home from school, before that big meeting, or while the police officer is walking toward your car. Remember, the benefits accumulate. As you become more relaxed and comfortable doing the complete breathing exercise, you will begin to find previously ingrained stressful, reactionary habits are automatically replaced by a refreshing breath. This allows you more oxygen to help you think and it also gives you a second or two to consider more healthy responses to any situation at hand.

After three months, do an assessment. You will undoubtedly find that these daily breathing exercises have positively affected you and your environment, including your home life, work life, friends, and, of course, your dog. If you see even a tiny change, make a mental progress note. It will encourage you to continue to refine your breathing and incorporate it more and more into your daily life.

Visualization for Experiencing Unconditional Love

A beautiful way to focus your energy is to send unconditional love to your dog—or to anything or anyone in your life. Recently, Christiane Northrup, M.D., a leading physician in the holistic health movement and author of *Women's Bodies, Women's Wisdom,* appeared on the Oprah Winfrey Show and demonstrated an exercise for unconditional love. The exercise is not new, but I was touched by Dr. Northrup's version of it—not only because she was teaching it on national television but also because she showed a slide of a puppy for the audience to focus on while doing the exercise. Dr. Northrup explained that it is scientific fact that this type of exercise "nourishes your heart" and creates the chemistry and physiology of peace and health in every cell of your body. She suggests doing this exercise for fifteen seconds two or three times a day. This exercise fits nicely into the nine ingredients of my holistic training program.

ILLUSTRATION 5

Visualizing or simply remembering something that triggers joy or peace will literally change your emotions and hence impact how you behave with and train your dog.

For this exercise, you'll need to focus on something or someone you love unconditionally. You can focus on this photo of a puppy or another photo or object of your choice. Or you can do this exercise with your eyes closed and focus on a person or object in your mind's eye.

1. Take one slow complete breath (Steps 1 and 2 of the complete breath exercise).
2. Now put your hand over your heart and think of unconditionally loving the person or object you selected for fifteen seconds or more.

How to Handle a Stress Crisis

So, what should you do when you come home after a bad day? Here you'll find stress management tools for you, the human half of the human-dog partnership. I've included both a quick stress management routine for emergency situations and a more in-depth routine that takes a bit more time and exploration. You can use the quick fix when the "stress overload truck" seems to be running you over.

Whichever stress management routine you opt to use, get the breathing down first so it becomes second nature. Implementing your stress management plan will give you a new perspective on the problem so you can consider the healthiest response. Along the way, with persistence and commitment, you will improve not only your stress management skills, but also your communication skills. Your dog will begin to understand what is expected of him and you will begin to understand what your dog is saying to you.

The first step in handling any stress overload is to get control of yourself. Remember, you can't expect a dog to be in control if you're out of control. As soon as you realize that you are out of control, follow one of the following formulas:

Quick Stress Management Routine for Humans

Stop, do one complete breath, tense your body, relax, do one more complete breath, and relax even more. Imagine the tension, anger, frustration—whatever—draining out of your muscles. Now apologize to your dog and give him a treat.

Complete Stress Management Routine for Humans

A. Physically stop whatever you are doing.
B. Stand still, briefly tense your body, then do the total relaxation exercise (see page 64) and complete breath exercise (see page 65).

C. Review the nine ingredients given in Chapter 2 to be sure all of your dog's needs are being met. With practice you will be able to do this in a few minutes.

D. Review the nine ingredients again with your own life in mind. Sometimes the best way to manage stress in your dog's life is to manage your own stress. Just as a dog's behavior can be impacted by an imbalance in the nine ingredients, so can a human's. Here are some examples:

1. *A High Quality Diet*: If your diet is not balanced, your body chemistry could be causing problems, leading to anxiety, depression, or crankiness. When did you eat last? Do you have low blood sugar? Are you wired because of an overload of caffeine?

2. *Play*: Have too many days gone by without having fun? Learn the two-step, go bowling, attend a concert.

3. *Socialization*: You're a human! Humans are supposed to be social. You not only need to spend time interacting with your own kind, you also need to challenge yourself from time to time. Play ball, play cards, go to a movie, or go out to dinner. And be sure to ask a friend or family member for support when you're troubled.

4. *Quiet Time*: When was the last time you took time for yourself? Take a walk, meditate, pray, or go to a museum.

5. *Exercise*: Exercise helps remove tension. Take a two-minute break from your work and do some stretching exercises. Work out, pump iron, do some yoga. And, as a special treat, get a massage.

6. *Employment*: Are you feeling fulfilled by your work? Employment doesn't just mean the place where you earn a living. Your "work" is all the ways you are productive or that you contribute to the world, including volunteer work. It includes such activities as baking cookies for a sick neighbor, coaching a Little League game, and walking a shelter dog.

7. *Rest*: Are you getting enough quality sleep? This seems to be an obvious point, yet if you ask a grumpy person why

he's grumpy, he'll often respond, "I didn't sleep well last night." Perhaps an afternoon nap is just what the doctor ordered.

8. *Training*: Training means pushing the boundaries of who you are physically, emotionally, and mentally—all under the greater spiritual umbrella. It means discipline in studying new subjects, maintaining your health, and striving for greater heights. What physical, mental, or spiritual disciplines have you added to your life recently? Pick one new element to add from time to time.

9. *Health Care*: Have you been ignoring a persistent health problem such as ongoing headaches, a nagging toothache, or depression? When you feel under the weather, you aren't in the best position to handle your dog and his needs. Make an appointment immediately with your physician, chiropractor, acupuncturist, nutritionist, dentist, mental health provider, or other practitioner.

E. If your training session is triggering your stress, review the eight tools of dog training given in Chapter 7 and decide which of the tools would best help with your dog's behavior in this situation. This only takes seconds. It's what great dog trainers do.

F. Implement your plan.

G. *Be sure to apologize to your dog for your inappropriate response.*

When you think about it, this stress management routine is really just common sense. It's the same commonsense stuff your mom and dad tried to communicate to you as you were growing up. When we're stressed, we sometimes forget the obvious. We forget we have the tools to help ourselves. So start with the smallest step. No one can plug all of these elements into his life at once. Nor should they. But, just like in dog training, you start at the point where you are. Begin at the point where you are already successful and build from there. I suggest starting by taking a deep breath!

chapter five

How to Speak "Dog"— Opening Doors of Communication

The Communication Gap

Years ago, when I was going to school in Mexico, my aunt and uncle traveled all the way from Cleveland to pay me a visit. For the most part, my uncle was a really nice guy. He used to be a milkman for those of you who remember having milk delivered to your door. Anyway, we were standing on a corner at Paseo de la Reforma. Rather than just asking me, he walked up to an elderly woman and said, "Can you tell us where the supermarket is?" The woman responded, *"Qué?"* So my uncle spoke louder. The woman took a few steps backward and said, "No speak English." She repeated this phrase several times. Finally my uncle returned. He was really mad. "Can you believe it?" he said. "She doesn't speak English."

My uncle's attitude illustrates the major stumbling block people have in communicating with their dogs. They actually think that they, being human, are lords and lordettes of the universe. It's an incredible, egotistical superiority complex. They expect their dogs to understand what they want. Instead of learning the language and customs of dogs, people do what my uncle did—speak louder and louder and say the same thing over and over—as if volume and repetition are going to suddenly bridge the communication gap. In short, they expect dogs to speak English. This ignorance comes out in statements like "stupid dog" or "He knows it, he's just being stubborn."

Picture yourself in a foreign country, unable to communicate. You don't know the body language or etiquette of the culture you're visiting. You might notice that everyone at the dinner table burps after the meal. If you don't know it's considered impolite *not* to burp, you will be considered a rude visitor. Or, you may offer someone your left hand, not knowing that it is considered offensive to do so. Then, all of a sudden, someone comes along who speaks to you in your own language and also explains the etiquette of the culture to you. Your relief would be almost palpable; the ability to communicate and be understood opens the world and all its wonders for you.

As explained in Chapter 3, dogs communicate with one another through tactile, tonal, and postural body language, which ranges from the very subtle to the very obvious. This body language can include a look or stare, blinking of the eyes, looking away, licking the lips, yawning, various speeds and locations of a wagging tail, sniffing the ground, scratching, mouthing, pawing, or marking the territory by urinating. Other body language includes the position of the body such as the play bow, turning the back or side to another dog, rolling over on the back, or blocking another dog's movement. Each movement is measured and exact—no more and no less than is absolutely necessary for the particular situation or moment of time. It's pure economy of motion.

ILLUSTRATION 6

In this photo, both the dogs and the people are saying hello in their own way. Notice how one dog is turning his head sideways, averting eye contact with the other dog.

Behaviors like these can be energy vents, helping to express built-up tension. As discussed in Chapter 3, these behaviors are called displacement behaviors. They are the result of competing motivators; that is, two desires that are pulling at the same time. Imagine, if you're a sports fan, being invited to see the Indians or the Browns, both playing on the same day at the same time. (Can you guess that I'm from Cleveland?) While you're trying to decide which game to attend, you might pace back and forth, or chew your nails, or eat something, or you might even feel a little stomach upset.

Dogs, as well as most other animals, have an amazing ability to notice the subtle movements made by other dogs as well as humans and associate these movements with consequences. The story of Hans the horse, which is well known in psychology circles, is a fascinating example of this ability to read subtle signals. Here is the story as it is related in Dr. Pam Reid's excellent book, *Excel-erated Learning:*

Clever Hans was a horse that belonged to Wilhelm von Osten in Germany back in the early 1900s. Von Osten believed he had taught his horse to do math. He would write arithmetic problems on a chalk board and Clever Hans would tap out the answer with his hoof. If von Osten wrote: 5 + 3 = Clever Hans would tap his foot against the floor 8 times.

The news of Clever Hans spread far and wide and eventually a group of scientists convened to study the horse. After watching a demonstration, they assigned a young student, Oskar Pfungst, to determine the extent of Hans's cleverness. Pfungst asked von Osten and his horse to undergo a series of tests. Pfungst asked von Osten to read Hans the question rather than write it down, he blindfolded Hans and asked von Osten to read him the question, he asked von Osten to show Hans a card with a problem written on it, he asked von Osten to show Hans a card with a question on it that von Osten himself hadn't seen, and so on. Through this battery of tests, Pfungst discovered that Hans could only answer the problems correctly if von Osten knew the answer. If von Osten didn't know the answer, neither did Clever Hans. In other words, von Osten was somehow cueing the horse, whether intentionally or unintentionally.

It was Pfungst's task to find out how. It turned out that Hans could answer the questions correctly as long as he could see von Osten but if von Osten was hidden from view, either behind a wall or even standing outside the periphery of Hans's vision, Hans was unable to answer. Pfungst had other people in to ask questions of Hans and he still answered correctly. Pfungst began observing von Osten very carefully and finally he hit on it: whenever von Osten (or anyone else, for that matter) asked Hans a question, von Osten's eyebrows lowered as he watched Hans tap his foot. As he completed the correct number of taps, von Osten lifted his eyebrows.

Pfungst tested his theory himself. Without saying a word to Hans, he lowered his eyebrows and sure enough Hans started tapping. Pfungst raised his eyebrows and Hans stopped tapping. Pfungst had solved the mystery of the clever horse!

The moral of the Clever Hans story is that things are not always what they seem. No matter how "obvious" something is, you never know for sure until you systematically rule out other explanations. And, in this case, a seemingly complex behavior had a very simple explanation. Caution was to become a cornerstone of the study of animal learning.[1]

Just like Clever Hans, dogs learn associations. They learn to connect events with a "what happens when" perspective. That's why it's so important to develop a "clean" precise body language of your own. Dogs can pick up on anything. What happens when you reach for the can in the closet? *I get fed.* What happens when the bell rings? *Someone comes in the door.* What happens when someone comes home, slams the door, and forcefully throws his coat on the chair? *I better hide so I don't get yelled at.* What happens when you put your coat on to leave for work? *I'm going to be left alone all day.* What happens when you put your coat on at night? *It's time to go for a walk.* Dogs can easily discriminate.

Because of the wide range of canine vocabulary, it's easy to see why most dogs are misread. People tend to anthropomorphize, giving

[1] Reid, Pamela, Ph.D., *Excel-erated Learning: Explaining How Dogs Learn and How Best to Teach Them,* James and Kenneth Publishers, 1996, pages 13–14.

their dogs human characteristics. "Oh, she peed on the bed *because she was mad at me.*" "*She was jealous* because I was hugging my boyfriend, so she bit him." Or, "She knew that knocking over the kitchen wastebasket was wrong *because she acted so guilty.*"

The extent to which people not only misread canine body language but have become inured to it was demonstrated by an incident shown on the television show *America's Funniest Home Videos*. Someone actually placed a defenseless little Chihuahua on a clothesline where she hung by her front paws. The dog's tail was between her legs, her ears were back against her head, and her entire body was shuddering. Then she began to urinate. The audience responded by howling in laughter at this poor scared little dog who was urinating out of fear. It's hard for me to imagine why people would think abusing this dog was funny. These are all examples of people who are unable to properly read the causes of the behavior because they just don't understand why dogs behave as they do or because they have become hardened to the point of insensitivity. When misperceptions lead to insensitivity, both animals and humans suffer. Education is the key to bridging the communication gap—and it also helps to open the heart to sensitivity and empathy.

Sometimes a dog's body language isn't very obvious. Just because a tail is wagging, that doesn't mean a dog is friendly. And, conversely, just because the hackles are up, that doesn't always mean a dog is going to bite. All individual body language expressions—the movement and location of the ears, tail, eyes, head, and the stance of the body—have to be taken in the overall context. No one feature can be translated into what's going on in the dog's mind and emotions.

Dogs can and do move from one expression to another in microseconds. Depending on what's going on in the environment, one moment he might be fearful, the next relaxed, and a second later he might bite. It is well worth the effort to attend a few classes and learn the subtle language of canine communication from an experienced trainer.

Dog Etiquette—How to Greet a Dog

Here are some ways to use canine body language in everyday situations when greeting dogs you are meeting for the first time or dogs you don't know well.

1. Keep your breathing easy and relaxed.
2. Until the dog learns to relax or is trained to enjoy "greetings," don't approach her straight on. Instead, imagine a curve on the ground like the letter "C" and approach along that curve. Once you are close to her, turn to your side rather than facing the dog head-on.
3. When you stop to greet people while on a walk or at your front door, turn to your side. By doing this, your dog will look at the other person as less threatening.
4. Instead of approaching a dog, let the dog come to you. Avoid sudden movements.
5. When greeting a dog, keep your hand down by your side.
6. Once you determine that the dog isn't feeling threatened, approach to pet him with your hand *under the chin where he can see where your hand is going,* not over his body. Then pet him gently on the chest or on the side of the face, away from the ears and eyes. *Don't ever reach over the dog's body to pet him on the top of the head or back until you know him well and are sure he enjoys being petted there.*
7. Avoid eye contact.
8. Speak in a monotone friendly voice with a lower register, but not one that is too low or too harsh.
9. Sometimes a silent yawn will help calm a dog and communicate that you aren't a threat.

Children should be supervised when interacting with dogs, even when the dogs are members of their own family. Seventy-five percent of the dog bites sustained by children are by dogs familiar to them. In some cases, if a dog has food or a toy, and a child comes into his personal space, he may feel the need to protect it and that protection could manifest in biting. Dogs should be allowed to eat in peace but for safety purposes they should also be educated to allow family members to reach into their bowl at any time. It is also important that we teach children to respect dogs and not to tease them with food or toys.

Your Role in Your Dog's Life

The popular idea that one dog in the pack is "dominant" in all situations has contributed to a misleading concept which has been perpetuated by the authors of many mainstream dog training books. They use this theory to teach you to mandate your authority as the leader of your dog's pack—the boss, the head honcho, the big cheese, the numero uno. Woe to him if he doesn't obey. The most frequently repeated phrase in these books is, "You must always win when training your dog." If you think about it, the phrase "you must always win" conveys that there is a competition going on. And a competition means there is a "win-lose" mentality. How can you and your dog become a behavioral team when you are caught up in an environment of having to compete and win at all costs?

Dogs are social animals. When they were domesticated 100,000 years ago, we became part of their social order and along the way we became their guardians, caregivers, protectors, and guides, but I don't buy into the "one dog rules all" pack mentality. Until another term comes along, the best way to view your role in your dog's life is as a member of his family—and the dog as a member of your family. In nonviolent dog training, you are not out to compete or "win" anything. There are no "commands" and no threats. Instead, you give your dog "signals" and reinforce his correct "responses." You are learning from each other how to work together.

According to Dr. Karen Overall, many animal behaviorists believe that although each member of a group works in his own self interest, that self interest manifests in shared responsibilities. It would be abnormal for one animal to constantly *have to* demonstrate through force that he was dominant. In reality, each situation in the group dynamic entails a collaborative effort. In the wild, these social interactions are dependent on what's going on in the environment because success for the group is dependent on working together. Wolves, for example, have a complex communication system that includes constant signaling between members. We are still trying to translate their subtle language. We do know, however, that studies suggest the only situations that trigger an absolute rank hierarchy are around disasters or stressful situations relating to resources.

Animals defer to one another to keep their group safe, strong, and healthy. If one individual threatens the group's collaborative efforts by asserting himself in ways contrary to the group's well being, he is thrown out. There are many examples of animal packs ousting members who tried to rule by brute force. Wolves have banished individuals who constantly used undue physical force to exert their authority. Monkeys also have been shown to attack and oust brutish members who used their strength and size against other members of the group.

Behavioral scientists are helping us better understand ourselves and our world by their study of collaborative efforts within various species. The following story is a terrific example of how we humans can learn from nature—in this case, from geese:

THE GOOSE STORY

Next fall, when you see geese heading south for the winter, flying along in "V" formation, you might consider what science has discovered about why they fly that way.

As each bird flaps its wings, it creates an uplift for the bird immediately following.

By flying in a "V" formation, the whole flock adds at least 71 percent more flying range than possible if each bird flew on its own.

People who share a common direction and sense of community can get where they are going more quickly and easily because they are traveling on the thrust of one another.

When a goose falls out of formation, it suddenly feels the drag and resistance of trying to go it alone . . . and quickly gets back into formation to take advantage of the lifting power of the bird in front.

If we have as much sense as the goose, we will stay in formation with those who are headed the same way.

When the head goose gets tired, it rotates back in the wing and another goose flies point.

It is sensible to take turns doing demanding jobs, whether with people or with geese flying south.

Geese honk from behind to encourage those up front to keep up their speed.

> **What do we say when we honk from behind?**
> *Finally—and this is important—when a goose gets sick or is wounded by gunshot or falls out of formation, two other geese fall out with that goose and follow it down to lend help and protection. They stay with the fallen goose until it is able to fly or until it dies. Only then do they launch out on their own or with another formation to catch up with their group.*
> If we have the sense of a goose, we will stand by each other like that.

Parents understand the importance of protecting and educating their children. After all, the parenting role requires not just providing food, shelter, and clothing, but also setting boundaries. What you want the dog to do and the child to do is to take their cues about the appropriateness of their behavior from you and that is the context within which you guide and protect them. A child can't just run out into the middle of the street, undress himself in the supermarket, or take a toy from another child. In the best of circumstances, the parent acts as a loving, nonviolent guardian; he is the source and provider of safety and comfort, and he educates the child through the use of examples, boundaries, and limits. In the same way, you must educate and act as a loving, nonviolent, benevolent guardian in your dog's life.

Asking your dog to lie down before releasing him to go up the steps or out the door presents terrific everyday training opportunities. So does asking him to sit before being fed, or asking him to jump off the couch so he can be rewarded by getting back on the couch to sit with you. But asking for these behaviors and rewarding your dog is much different than "showing him who's boss" and forcing him to sit, lie down, and obey you in all things under the threat of punishment.

So ask yourself why you are teaching your dog to sit, lie down, and come when called. For safety purposes? Ideally, we train our dogs to respond to our signals so we can help them and ourselves be all that we can be. Training stimulates growth and forms a bond between us because it involves communication and interaction. A synergy emerges allowing both our dogs and ourselves to grow and learn in ways that are unique and might otherwise be impossible. I have learned as much, if not more, about patience, honesty, compassion, and congruity matching my words to my actions, thoughts, and emotions—in the companionship of dogs as I have in any other endeavor. In addition, I believe my dogs have also benefited in ways I can't even imagine.

So when you read about or hear about how important it is to control your dog by showing him who's boss, I ask that you reconsider. Don't compete; instead educate. Show him how the world provides his food, affection, and freedom—and ignores him when he behaves inappropriately. (Of course, use common sense here—don't ignore him when doing so would cause harm to him, to others, or to the environment.) Educate your dog about the appropriateness of his behavior. Create an environment in which you can guide and protect him, yourself, and the environment.

Dr. Karen Overall, director of the Behavior Clinic of the School of Veterinary Medicine at the University of Pennsylvania, sums up the path to a great relationship with our dogs with the following overview:

- Practice deferential behaviors.

- Do not use physical punishment.

- Teach the dog that you are not a threat.

- Reward good behaviors, even when they are spontaneous.

- Don't worry about minor details—none of us are perfect.

- Always let the dog know he can have treats, love, or toys if he sits quietly first.

- Never do something just because you can.

- Talk to your dog. Use his or her name. Signal clearly.

- Be reliable and trustworthy.

Opening More Subtle Doors of Communication

Almost all of us have had hunches that proved true. Have you ever received a call from a person you were just planning to call, had the same brilliant idea as another person, or had a sudden intuitive understanding of what an animal wants? One of the strangest experiences I've had happened in 1979. I was with a friend in India when a complete stranger came up and told him a number of things he had no way of knowing. The stranger told my friend, "Your girlfriend's name is Sue; you live in Cleveland, Ohio; you are an engineer; and your birthday is on the second of January." He went on to tell my friend his mother's name and a few other details of his life most of his friends didn't even know.

On another occasion, an Indian mystic told me, "Your mother recently had a terrible upset and you moved back in with her to take care of her." He was right, my mother had recently divorced and I had moved back in with her. Then he said, "You were very sick as a boy with lung problems and your twin sister has a back problem." Both statements were true. He proceeded to draw some lines that looked like railroad tracks on a piece of paper. "This is the spine. Here is her problem." It was true; she did have a back problem. And then he pointed to the exact vertebra that was causing her trouble. At no time did he ask me any questions. I know of yet another incident in which a teacher who spoke no English suddenly understood everything that was said to him and even answered questions in English.

In all of these situations, a person is linked to information and abilities that he seemingly has no direct access to. Most of us would call this person psychic. Webster defines the word "psychic" as "beyond natural or known physical processes." In Eastern philosophy, this is called "direct knowing," which is the ability to directly access information without having to learn it from an outside source or through what most people would consider normal means. In other words, the information is just there—downloaded, so to speak, into your reality without the need to attend a lecture, read a book, or use any other method of learning. We all do this to one extent or another.

Edgar Mitchell, the Apollo 14 astronaut who was the sixth person to walk on the moon, shares the following experience he had in space, which he describes as life-altering: "As I approached the planet we know as home, I was filled with an inner conviction as certain as any mathematical equation I'd ever solved. I suddenly knew . . . that the beautiful blue world to which we were returning is part of a living system, harmonious and whole; and that we all participate in a universe of consciousness." He goes on to say: "I became convinced that the uncharted territory of human consciousness was the next frontier to explore, that it contained possibilities we had hardly begun to imagine."[2] As far as I'm concerned, anyone who is reading this book is part of this next frontier Mitchell is talking about.

In Dr. Michael Fox's book *Superdog*, an entire chapter deals with animal telepathy and extrasensory perception. One amazing true story details the journey of two dogs and a cat that traveled across the country to a place they'd never even visited, to be with their relocated humans. How is this possible? In addition, how do dogs seemingly predict our comings and goings and do other out-of-the-ordinary stuff? And how can you learn to, in essence, read your dog's mind? Welcome to the world of subtle communication, intuition, and psychically derived knowledge.

So why am I presenting this information in a book on dog training? Well, it's fun, for one thing. For another, if we set limits on what's possible, we are only limiting our own potential. It also introduces one of the most powerful tools a dog trainer has at his disposal—learning to shut up and listen. When your mind is going a mile a minute, your thoughts keep you so preoccupied that you often miss what's right in front of you. It is only when you are centered and focused and your mind is quiet that the subtle realms of communication are open to you.

If you choose to explore these matters and, for instance, telepathically teach your dog to sit, you can experiment with the method that follows. At the very least, there is something to be said about developing your intuitive awareness as a tool to help keep your dog safe and healthy. I submit that dogs are not here for our amusement or to serve us. Maybe we're here to serve them. Maybe if we raise a dog to be all that she can be, whatever that is, we are helping ourselves to be all that we can be as humans. That's what this book is about—discovery. Don't limit what you can do with your dog and don't limit what your dog can do.

There are several methods to develop your direct reception of information and utilize the more subtle aspects of awareness. Eastern philosophy says this ability is due to karma and a direct result of cause and effect. According to other philosophies, these abilities are simply gifts from God.

When I was in Aspen back in the '70s, I got a job working in a restaurant as a short-order cook. I decided to experiment with this

---

[2] Mitchell, Edgar, Membership Letter from Institute for Noetic Sciences, February, 1999, page 1.

technique by guessing what people would order. So, before the customers even ordered, I would throw hamburgers on the grill and drop fries and chicken in the basket. I must say I got pretty good at guessing what people were going to order. The waiter would drop the ticket off and thirty seconds later the lunch would be served. It was really funny seeing the look on the faces of the waiters and the customers. Some of the customers returned day after day because of the unbelievably fast service. But then, after a couple of weeks of almost perfect hunches, I found my guesses going sour. I'd have six or seven hamburgers frying and no one to eat them. Suddenly, my intuitive information was no longer flowing. The problem? A thought crept in that I was really good at this. Once my ego was involved, it was as if I started to "possess" the ability and the information no longer flowed. The trick to tapping into the more subtle aspects of communication starts with getting your ego out of the way. Fun is one thing; a power trip is another.

Practice the following exercise before every training session and you will see synergy at work. Your intuitive ability to communicate with your dog will evolve tremendously.

Communication Exercise
Note: It is not necessary to spend more than ninety seconds on this exercise.

1. Open your awareness by closing your eyes and doing three rounds of the complete breath exercise. (See page 65.) Listen to the sound of your breathing.
2. Tense all the muscles in your body at once. Hold for three seconds and then relax and let your body go limp.
3. Do one more round of the complete breath exercise.
4. Now open your eyes and become an observer. Watch yourself watching your dog. Do this by pretending you are in a movie and watching the movie at the same time. "Feel" your dog's mood, attitude, and energy level. The key here is to quiet your own mind so you can really tune in to what's going on with your dog. It's important to do this from your intuition, not your intellect. This process takes only seconds. Now you're plugged in to

nature's rhythms. It's that easy. The more you concentrate and the more you rely on your subtle observational skills, the more accurately you'll be able to communicate with your dog.

5. Think about each of the behaviors you are going to work on in the upcoming session. With your eyes closed, spend ten seconds picturing your dog in the final position of each behavior. For example, picture your dog in a sit position for ten seconds, then a down position for ten seconds, and so on. Really use your imagination and focus in your mind's eye on each separate behavior; infuse each behavior with the power of your will. You do this by really imagining it as real. The more you can make it real, the quicker the behavior will take shape.

The technique of picturing the result in your mind's eye is the same one used by world class athletes in both training and competition. People in my classes have reported some pretty amazing results when they take the time before each training session to do this simple exercise. You should notice progress within three weeks of steady practice. To accelerate the results even more, some people do this mental exercise not only before each training session but also at other times during the day, whenever they happen to remember. The more you practice, the greater the results.

chapter six

How Dogs Learn

There are three ways to nonviolently train your dog:

1. Simply wait for the behavior to occur, then let the dog know that what he just did thrilled you to no end by rewarding him with praise, a scratch behind the ear, and treats.
2. Use a visual prompt such as food, a favorite toy, or other object to lure the dog to do what you want, then praise and reward.
3. Use a physical prompt like gently pushing the dog's behind on the floor to get him to sit, then praise and reward him.

The training in this book deals exclusively with methods 1 and 2. In this chapter you'll learn why it's so easy to get your dog to do what you want him to do. It's simply a matter of applying some simple principles and being consistent. Consistency means that everyone who interacts with the dog follows the same training guidelines and methods.

Classical Versus Operant Conditioning

There's a story about an elderly woman who, around seven one night, reached for her walking cane and called her two dogs to go for a walk. As the dogs raced in from the yard, they both spied the cane. One dog jumped up, wagged his tail, and couldn't wait to go outside. The other dog, recently obtained from the local shelter, became distressed. His ears lay flat, his shoulders went down, his tail dropped between his legs, he began to lick his lips and pant, and finally urinated as the woman started to walk toward him with the cane. "What's the matter, Sparky?" the woman gently asked. "We're just going for a walk."

Here we have one cane and two very different reactions. This cane, a simple piece of wood, meant something completely different to each dog. Why? Association. The first dog had a history of pleasant experiences with the cane; it meant that he got to go for a walk, visit his friends, say hello to the neighborhood. The second dog had a history too. He had previously lived with a family that would whack him with a stick whenever they felt like it—mostly for urinating on the carpet. To this dog, a cane meant trouble.

Back in the 1930s, the famous behaviorist Ivan Pavlov discovered that when dogs learned to associate the sound of a bell with food, they would salivate every time a bell rang. After a while, whether food was present or not, the dogs would still salivate when the bell was rung. This kind of learning is called classical conditioning, also known as respondent conditioning. The word "conditioning" simply means learning.

In classical conditioning the dog learns to associate. He learns that if "A" happens, then "B" will happen. But the results are not contingent upon what he does. In other words, some event will happen one way or another, no matter how he responds. The bell rings, food appears, and the resultant behavior is salivation. This type of conditioning happens in our own lives, too. For instance, when you see the lights of a police car flashing in your rear-view mirror, you get a ticket. The result is that every time you see a police car you have heart palpitations and sweaty palms.

Classical conditioning can be used to empower your dog training clicker (which I'll discuss later in this chapter) so it becomes as valuable as a reward. If you link or associate food with praise, you increase the value of your praise. And if you say "good" whenever you give your dog a piece of turkey, over time the word "good" will become as good as the turkey. Or, whenever a leash appears, you take your dog for a walk. Over time he learns to associate the leash with something "good," and as a result he always gets excited. This will be reflected internally by a faster heartbeat and flowing adrenaline and outwardly by his excited jumping.

Operant conditioning, on the other hand, is conditioning or learning in which the consequence *is* contingent upon the behavior. To make it simple, it follows the ABC principle.

The ABC's of Operant Conditioning

Each of the behaviors in the chart below is learned by the principles of operant conditioning.

ILLUSTRATION 7

A. The Antecedent (any sensory stimulation) that signals →	B. The Behavior (anything your dog does) in anticipation of →	C. The Consequence (something the dog receives after performing the behavior)
A *sound*, such as: The word "sit" signals →	Putting the behind on the floor in anticipation of →	Receiving a food treat.
A ringing bell signals →	Running to the mat in anticipation of →	Getting to go outside.
The footsteps of a person approaching the house signals→	Running to the door and barking in anticipation of →	Receiving praise.
A *touch*, such as: Being touched on the paw signals →	Raising the paw as in "let's shake hands" in anticipation of →	Getting to chase a ball.
Being patted on the head signals →	Jumping on the couch in anticipation of →	Getting to be with you.
A *smell*, such as: Dog food signals →	Running to the kitchen and lying down in anticipation of →	Dinner being served.
Cologne signals →	Running to the door to greet a favorite person in anticipation of →	Receiving praise and petting from the visitor.
Illegal drugs signal →	Barking to announce the presence of drugs in anticipation of →	Receiving praise and more food.

Motivation

Several factors influence learning. But to keep it simple, when we talk about motivation, it means dogs do stuff because there's something in it for them. "Show them the money!" What you want to do is elevate yourself in your dog's eyes so no matter what, you're it. You are the prime motivator.

When you first start training your dog, what happens when you yell "sit"-while a squirrel runs through the yard? Where's the $10,000? At that moment in time, chasing the squirrel is the $10,000 payoff. If the next-door neighbor's female dog is in heat and your unneutered male hears you yelling "come," where's the $10,000? It's the female, of course. Chasing squirrels, greeting mail carriers, meeting other dogs, and smelling road kill are all powerful motivators that distract your dog's attention from what you are asking him to do. In these situations, you, the erstwhile provider of all things good in your dog's universe, have taken a back seat. Therefore, in order to get your dog to do what *you* want, you need to become worth more than the distractions.

In nonviolent dog training both classical and operant conditioning are used. You can increase the value of your praise or affection by initially linking it with a primary reinforcer, like food. *This is classical conditioning.* You can also elevate yourself as a motivator by creating an environment where your dog has to come to you to get anything he wants. You control the food, affection, toys, social freedom, climate control, and everything else in his universe. There is no negotiation. In effect, you are saying, "I'll give you the world, but you've got to do something for me first." *This is operant conditioning.*

In human terms, think of a Las Vegas slot machine, the lottery, or horse racing. In all of these cases there are great rewards, good rewards, and average rewards. Who's got the power to release these rewards? Who's the motivator? In the dog's Las Vegas mentality, one dog might consider a piece of raw liver as a $10,000 reward, while another dog, at times, might consider a squeaky toy the highest reward possible.

Primary ($10,000) rewards: Special food treats
Secondary rewards: Affection through praise and touching
     Play, including toys
     Social interaction, including allowing
       your dog to go places with you
       such as a ride in the car, walk-
       ing up and down the stairs,
       going in and out of doors, or
       being allowed on the bed or
       other furniture

Whatever the reward, you are the one to control it. You are the prime motivator.

Context Learning

Did you ever find yourself in a situation where someone came up to you and greeted you and you were totally stumped about who they were? You knew that you knew the person but you couldn't associate the face with how you knew him. We've all had this kind of experience. You know someone from work or church or the PTA, but when you run into him at the supermarket or on the street, you just can't quite put your finger on who he is or how you know him. What you're experiencing is situational or context learning. You know the person from one context or situation in your life and he's suddenly appeared in another context. The same thing happens in dog training.

Mike, who believed that his golden retriever, Sunny, was the smartest dog in the Western world, taught him all sorts of tricks. He taught Sunny to sit, play dead, crawl, shake hands, roll over, and balance a biscuit on his nose. One night, while watching *Buffy, the Vampire Slayer,* Mike saw a commercial where a dog opened a refrigerator, grabbed a can of beer, and brought it to his handler. Mike decided that Sunny could do that. So, he taught him to open the refrigerator, get a can of beer, bring it to him, sit quietly by while he drank it, and then take the empty can and ceremoniously deposit it in the wastebasket.

It took several weeks but finally Sunny had the trick down pat. Mike couldn't wait to have his friends over for Superbowl Sunday so he could show off Sunny performing this amazing feat. With the masses gathered and in high anticipation, Mike confidently instructed Sunny to "get me a beer." Sunny jumped up and down, wagged his tail, barked excitedly, and did every trick in the book except going to get the beer. You can imagine the heckling from Mike's buddies. What Mike didn't understand was that Sunny had no idea what Mike was asking of him because he had been trained to do this behavioral sequence in an environment with no distractions. Mike never trained him with ten people hanging around. That new context formed a kind of "excitement wall"—blocking his memory.

Mike's experience illustrates the idea of context learning. When you teach a dog to sit in the living room with no one else around, that doesn't mean he'll remember what you want when you ask him to sit outside in the yard. Not only are there more distractions outside, which is part of the "context," but the grass—where he's being asked to put his behind—is also a new factor. Then when you add friends, other animals, various noises, and other sundry distractions, your dog needs time to regroup and assimilate each change. Always build on your dog's successful performances. As he becomes more and more successful, begin asking for duration, increasing the distance, or adding distractions. Eventually he'll "generalize" and perform the expected behavior wherever and whenever you request it.

Shaping a Behavior

Shaping a behavior means rewarding one baby step after another baby step until you have shaped the final behavior you want. This is done through the use of "successive approximations." In other words, each rewarded baby movement is a part of—or an approximation of—the final goal. Reward all successive behaviors that lead to the final behavioral goal. Confused? Hang on.

Shaping a dog's behavior is like the game of "hot and cold," in which the person who is "it" tries to determine which object in the room the other players have selected for him to find. He moves around the room while the other players say "You're getting warm" and "Now you're getting colder" until finally the person gets close to the object he's supposed to find and is told, "You're red-hot!" It's just the same with a dog. Each time your dog gets closer to doing what you want, reward his efforts with praise and treats. When he gets further away from the behavior you want, ignore the behavior—which is the same as saying "You're getting cold." Then, when he finally "gets it," he receives a jackpot—several $10,000 rewards.

You can shape virtually any behavior you want from your dog, including wagging his tail at various speeds, a very fast or a very slow sit, sneezing three times in a row, or nodding his head yes and no. All of these behaviors are simply shaped and molded one step at a time.

Here's another example: To shape your dog's behavior to sit up in the begging position, first reward her for sitting. Then, hold the treat a little higher and reward her for stretching up or craning her neck to get the treat. Then reward her again when she lifts one paw off the ground; again when she lifts two paws off the ground; and finally reward only the finished balanced pose.

In nonviolent training, we use three ways to shape behavior: positive reinforcement, negative reinforcement, and negative punishment. Scientifically speaking, a reinforcement, whether positive or negative, increases the likelihood of a behavior being repeated and punishment decreases the likelihood. To help you understand the principles behind all of these ways to shape your dog's behavior, I will give you a brief description and example of each of them. However, in nonviolent training, positive reinforcement is used the most. Occasionally some negatives are used in nonviolent training, but only when they do not harm the dog or the human physically, emotionally, or mentally.

Positive reinforcement means rewarding behaviors you want your dog to repeat. When your dog performs the sit behavior, reward him for it. Give him a treat every time he puts his behind on the floor, and there's a good chance he'll keep putting his behind on the floor. Give a child $10 every time she gets an "A" on her report card and there's a good chance she'll continue getting good grades. Again, this is one of the primary ways to shape your dog's behavior in nonviolent dog training.

Negative reinforcement means taking something bad away in order to get her to do something. While it is possible to use negative reinforcement nonviolently, some people use aversive methods including shocking, shaking, ear pinching, and continual jerking. If you use any of these methods, you are saying to your dog, "I'm only going to stop hurting you when you pick up that ball." For us, the seat belt alarm in a car is a form of negative reinforcement. Until you snap the seat belt together, the irritating buzzer continues to sound. The age-old silent treatment is also a form of negative reinforcement. Your significant other's refusal to speak to you is a negative (well, in this case) and until you apologize, you're in the doghouse. In this book we occasionally present negative reinforcement methods, but only when it does not harm the dog.

Punishment means doing something to decrease the likelihood your dog will ever repeat a particular behavior again. People punish their dogs by hitting, kicking, shocking, shaking, swatting with newspapers, and so on to try to stop behaviors like jumping, pulling on a leash, stealing food, mouthing, etc. Punishment also means taking something good away from your dog to get him to *stop* doing a behavior. If your puppy bites you, you walk away. If you ask your dog to sit but he barks instead, you eat the treat that was intended for him. The human equivalent would be taking away your child's computer or phone privileges to stop him from coming home late. This is called negative punishment because you are *taking something away* from your dog. In this case, the word "negative" means removing.

The Steps to Shaping a Behavior

1. Get a picture firmly planted in your own mind of the behavior you want from your dog. Remember, if you don't know what you want your dog to do, she can't figure it out either. According to interspecies communicator Samantha Khury, the best way to do this is to visualize the goal—for instance, the dog sitting—in the same way you visualize when you daydream or fantasize. In other words, make it as real as you can.
2. Get your dog's attention by using a sound, a motion, or some other lure such as a food treat or your dog's favorite squeaky toy. (We'll cover more on lures later in this chapter.)
3. Add steps to the behavior one at a time. Reward even the smallest parts (approximations) of the behavior that you think will lead to the final goal. Don't go too fast or too slowly. If your dog

is losing interest or getting distressed, you've gone too far too fast. Back up and get her attention again and set it up so she's successful.

4. Establish one part of the behavior, such as a sit without distractions, before adding another one, such as a sit with distractions, following the reinforcement schedules. (See Reinforcement Schedules on page 103.) Once your dog has mastered one part of the behavior, she is then ready to move on to the next part. You'll know the time is right to move to the next part of the behavior when you only have to reward your dog every once in a while because she is doing the behavior repeatedly—or at least 80 percent of the time. If your dog is confused, once again, you've gone too far, too fast. Back up to the point where your dog was successful and work that step for a while, then ask for more again.

The Repetition Factor: The only way your dog will learn to do something reliably is to have him repeat the behavior over and over. There are no shortcuts. Depending on the dog's age, genetic predisposition, motivation level, ability, lifestyle, etc., the repetition factor can range from several hundred to over ten thousand repetitions of any one behavior over a period of months or years. The degree of reliability is directly related to the number of successful responses in various environments. Professional trainers view the ages of between two and four years old as the stage when reliability sets in. A good comparison is teaching a young child to tie his shoes, eat with a fork, or dress himself. It takes time and patience.

Biorhythms and Learning Curves

Common sense dictates that dogs have good days and bad days just as we do. Emotionally and physically they just might be feeling a little low or anxious one day and really motivated the next. What works in the morning might not work in the evening. What works in a low distraction environment won't work in a busy environment. What works when a dog is feeling well might not work if she is suffering from a digestive upset or if an arthritic condition is acting up.

Just like humans, dogs have their own biorhythm cycles. Physically, emotionally, and mentally, they learn on a roller coaster–like curve—integrating more and more information, gradually reaching higher, then going down a little, then reaching higher than before. One day he enthusiastically sits every time you request it and the next day he acts as if he never heard the word. The trick to being a really great instructor is learning when your dog is "up" and when it's time to back off in training, so you will be nurturing and challenging him at his own learning rate.

In a strictly controlled environment, like a laboratory or a marine mammal water park, learning curves are plotted and vigilantly followed for optimum results. But in an everyday, typical harried home, who has the time? Most people feel it's the dog's job to fit into the human's schedule and lifestyle. I agree with this notion—but not at the expense of the health and welfare of the dog, which means taking into account how the dog is feeling physically, mentally, and emotionally. After all, how your dog is feeling directly relates to the success of your training program. Developing your observational skills and intuition plays a big part in helping this process along.

Remember that dogs are on dog time—they live in the present. Their attention can be diverted in a split second. It may be riveted on you one second, and in the next, distracted by the slightest sight, sound, touch, or smell. Taking this into consideration, as well as your own busy lifestyle, all you need to do is take ninety seconds to tune into your dog both mentally and physically before you begin a training session. You can do this by practicing the communication exercise on page 85.

Lures, Bribes, and Rewards

A *lure* is a promise of a reward. It is a piece of food or other item that entices your dog to do what you want. For instance, if your dog is hungry and you put a piece of turkey in front of his nose, you can use it to lure him to follow you. Squeaky toys can be lures, a can of dog food can be a lure, and opening the front door can lure your dog to see what's up.

On the other hand, a *bribe* is a lure gone astray. If you have to show your dog a piece of turkey every time you want him to do something, you're bribing him. A lure is used only to get him interested, and then, only if it's necessary. If you find yourself dependent upon food or toys in order to get your dog to do something, you can bet that you are using these things as bribes. Once your dog is motivated to do the behavior you are asking for, you need to stop luring him and only reward him.

A *reward*, as the term is used in this book, is a positive reinforcement. A reinforcement is a reward for desired behavior. Unlike a lure, which is used to *get* your dog interested in doing something, a reward is something you give him after he has performed the desired behavior. When you give your dog a piece of turkey as soon as his behind hits the floor, you are rewarding him. Never bribe a dog. Instead, interrupt his thinking and entice him in other ways. Once your dog knows something good is associated with his behavior, you don't have to keep showing it to him.

Rewards have a pecking order. Some are great, some good, some just okay. To keep your dog highly motivated, especially when teaching a new exercise or behavior, always use a great reward—one that's worth $10,000 in human terms. But there's a caution involved here. Rewards have to *keep* their value. If the same great reward is given over and over again, it will lose its value. Also, if you give too much of the same reward at any one time, it can lose its value. The classic example of this point is the story of the trainer who guaranteed she could get a dog to ignore a freshly cooked steak without resorting to any negative training. How? Shortly before the demonstration she simply gave the dog more steak than he could possibly eat. Then, when it came time for the demonstration, she offered him yet another piece and he ignored it. The steak had lost its value because the dog couldn't eat another bite.

Like the above example, other rewards, such as praise, can also be misused and lose their power. Of course, you want to praise your dog consistently. However, your dog should earn that praise. If you give your dog praise all the time for doing nothing, he may begin to ignore you. The same goes for your dog's favorite toys. They, too, should be rewards for doing what you've asked, rather than something that's always available. Rewards—to be rewards—have to keep their value.

Make sure you only use great $10,000 rewards when you are teaching a new behavior or when you begin to shape that behavior as described earlier in this chapter on page 92. Of course, you can cheat a little and occasionally give a $10,000 treat just for the heck of it, because he's such a great dog and you're a wonderful person.

The 80 Percent Rule—How to Make Your Words Mean Something

There were two sets of twins, and five children in all, in my home when I was growing up. As typical kids we'd be upstairs at bedtime jumping up and down on the beds, giggling, and making all sorts of racket when we were supposed to be going to sleep. My parents would yell from downstairs, "If I have to come upstairs . . ." But we'd go on giggling and romping.

Eventually my father would take the threat even further. He'd pretend he was coming upstairs by standing at the bottom of the stairs and making stomping noises. That didn't get us to quiet down either. We had learned that our parents' threats were irrelevant. They didn't have any power because they were all empty threats. It would take nine or ten threats before there would be any serious action on my parents' part to stop our inappropriate behavior. Finally, my dad would actually come up the stairs. Then we'd really shut up, dive under the covers, and pretend we were asleep, hoping he couldn't hear the pounding of our hearts.

Dogs learn the same way as humans do. Words are irrelevant unless they have power behind them and really mean something. Words will have power if you link them with consequences, like receiving a reward, and that introduces us to the 80 percent rule. That is, when to label a behavior to make it mean something and when to add duration, distance, and distractions to your training.

Throughout the lessons in Part II, we will refer to the 80 percent rule: When you are 80 percent sure your dog will do such and such, move on to the next level. The way to know when your dog is ready to go on to something else is based on your judgment. You know your dog better than anybody. The rule of thumb, however, is this: If your dog does what you're asking eight out of ten times in any particular situation, move on.

Some behaviors, such as sit and lie down, must be established before you can label them. In other words don't say "sit" unless you're sure she'll sit. These behaviors are first taught using hand motions, clickers, lures, and rewards. When do you start saying the word "sit"? When she sits eight out of ten times, it is time to label the behavior by saying "sit" immediately preceding the hand motion. Now she will begin to associate putting her behind on the floor with the word "sit."

Other behaviors, however, can be labeled immediately because you're already 80 percent sure your dog will respond. Examples of this are stay, come when called, go to your spot, and asking your dog to touch either a stick or your hand. In these behaviors, your dog figures out what you want very quickly, because she's simply following the treat. If you're using a target stick and you have your dog's attention, you can also label whatever behavior you're working on immediately. For example, when you want your dog to stay, your hand blocks her from moving forward and the reward comes in split seconds, so she is immediately successful. The same holds true for "go to your spot." She follows the treat to the spot, so she's already doing the behavior.

But remember, when you begin teaching any new behavior, you must be in a nondistracting environment AND you must have your dog's attention, which is where the $10,000 lure comes in. You can only say "stay" in an environment or situation in which you are 80 percent sure she'll respond. Motivation is the key. You cannot *say* "stay," "come," or "go to your spot" if the environmental distractions are greater than you. In other words, following the 80 percent rule, if your dog is looking at a raccoon, you can't say "come" because you know your dog won't come. *Only* use a signal when you're 80 percent sure your dog will respond. You may be able to get your dog to come when called inside the house, but outdoors with a raccoon nearby is another story. You must gradually progress in each behavior to make your dog more and more reliable, by adding the three Ds (duration, distance, and distractions—see page 101) one at a time.

There is no such thing as 100 percent reliability. Factors such as illness, injury, accumulated stress, age, what you have trained for, and so on affect your dog's reliability. If your dog responds 80 percent of the time on any one behavior, you should consider it reliable behavior. If your dog gives you the behavior you are asking for 90 percent of the time, in different environments, that is considered very reliable. This degree of reliability is known in the dog training world as being under "stimulus control," or in simpler terms, you've got an obedience trained dog.

Teach Your Dog to Sit Before Labeling It "Sit"

Note: I realize the following is not the perfect methodology for purists in the applied animal behavior field, but in my experience, it makes training much more accessible for many dog enthusiasts.

As mentioned before, some behaviors can be labeled immediately while others should not be labeled until the behavior is established. Don't say "sit" or "down" until the behavior is already established and you are 80 percent sure your dog will sit or lie down. Here are the steps to labeling a behavior, using "sit" as an example. (The full instructions for teaching "sit" are on page 153 in Part II of this book.)

The Steps to Labeling a Behavior

1. Start in a nondistracting environment. Use a $10,000 piece of food as a lure and make the hand signal for "sit."
2. After numerous repetitions, when you're 80 percent sure your dog will sit when you use the hand signal, put the food in the other hand. Now make the hand signal, click as soon as your dog sits and reward from the other hand for each successful repetition. (As discussed in the section on lures, bribes, and rewards, you're now using the exact same food as a reward. It is no longer a lure.)
3. When you are 80 percent sure your dog will sit when you make the hand motion for "sit" without using food, it's at *that* moment you label the behavior by saying "sit" immediately preceding the hand movement. Then repeat this a thousand times or however long it takes, rewarding each successful response.
4. When you are 80 percent sure that you will get what you're looking for, begin to add the three Ds—duration, distance, and distractions—which you'll learn in the next section.

An alternative to the four steps listed is to simply use a target. You don't have to wait to label the behavior if your dog has already learned to target something like your hand or a target stick. In that case, you can skip steps 1, 2, and 3, and begin labeling the behavior immediately before presenting the target. Once again, you must start in a nondistracting environment. (If this sounds confusing, don't worry. You'll learn how to use a target on page 108.)

> *The 80 Percent Rule: If your dog does a particular behavior eight out of ten times, it's a good bet that he is ready for you to up the ante and ask for more. Never ask for a behavior unless you're 80 percent sure your dog will do it in any given situation.*

For many behaviors, labeling them *after* your dog has learned them is extremely important insofar as giving your signal word power. This is where many handlers get confused. They repeat "sit," "sit," "sit" over and over with no results. Their words simply have no power. Just as with my parents, yelling at my brother and sisters and me to go to sleep, the word you're using to signal a behavior becomes totally irrelevant to the dog. Other people make the mistake of saying "sit" *after* the dog has already sat. The word "sit" should be the signal to sit, not something you say *after* the dog is already in position.

Another classic example of irrelevant and unintentional training is yelling "come" as the dog runs across the street chasing a squirrel. If you say the word "come" often enough while your dog is running away from you, she might begin to think the word "come" means run the other way. After all, that's when she hears it the most. To make the word you're using *relevant*, don't use it unless you're 80 percent sure your dog will actually do what you're asking.

The 3 Ds—Adding Duration, Distance, and Distractions to the Training Process

Once your dog has learned to do a basic behavior, such as "sit," in a low distraction environment and she sits when you ask her at least 80 percent of the time, she is ready to move on to new levels of "sit." It's time to gradually add the three Ds: duration, distance, and distractions.

1. *Duration* is added first by asking her to sit for longer and longer periods of time.
2. Next, add *distance* by asking her to sit from a greater and greater distance.
3. Finally, add an increasing number of *distractions*. For example, train your dog to sit outdoors, then with other people around, then with other dogs around, etc.

You always begin with duration and then add the other variables separately. If you're asking your dog to sit for longer periods of time, don't simultaneously introduce distance and start walking away. Duration is one thing, distance is another. And, if you're working on distance and asking your dog to sit while you walk away, don't add duration at the same time by asking him to stay in that position for a longer period of time.

Similarly, when you are teaching a behavioral sequence like getting a soda from the refrigerator, each behavior in the sequence is taught individually in an environment without distractions. Then the entire package or series of behaviors making up the trick must be practiced and linked together with more and more distractions, for shorter or longer periods of time, and/or at greater distances.

Whenever you add another factor to the training process, whether it is the length of time she is asked to do the behavior, your distance from her while she's doing it, or distractions while she's doing it, always add them individually, one at a time.

In the lessons in Part II of this book, most behaviors are taught in four different levels. Each behavior starts at the beginner's level. Then you gradually add duration, distance, and distractions as you proceed through the levels. Based on your dog's progress, you will know when to go from Level 1 to Level 2, and so on.

Reinforcement Schedules

Professional trainers and behaviorists use training schedules that dictate when and how often to reward your dog. These reinforcement schedules, as they are called, can be quite complex—and they are strictly adhered to. This book introduces only a general application of these rules by way of a three-step process:

Step 1: *A continuous reinforcement schedule.* When you begin training for any behavior, it's important to reward your dog each and every time he responds to your signal, e.g., sit, *treat*, sit, *treat*, sit, *treat*, etc. For simple behaviors in a nondistracting environment, a few hundred repetitions spread out over several days or weeks may be all that's necessary for your dog to grasp what's going on. You'll also revert to this schedule whenever you add duration, distance, or distractions to each behavior.

Step 2: *A variable reinforcement schedule.* At the next stage of training, instead of rewarding the dog after every response, he is rewarded on a predetermined schedule, such as after every second, third, or fourth response (sit, sit, *treat*,—or sit, sit, sit, sit, *treat*), or after two, three, or more *different* behaviors, e.g., sit, down, sit, *treat*, etc.

Step 3: *An intermittent or random reinforcement schedule.* In this stage, you progress to rewarding every so often, like the occasional win in Las Vegas. Once the dog knows that a payoff is coming sooner or later, he will remain motivated.

Following these progressions will take you a long way toward your goal of obtaining reliable behavior with your dog. Learning when to go from one reinforcement schedule to another is what makes a good trainer. Some dogs learn more quickly than others; go too slowly with those dogs and they quickly become bored. Other dogs need to remain on one schedule for a longer period of time; if you go too fast, they become stressed and you end up having to retrace your steps. The trick is learning how to use these schedules in order to challenge your dog and progress at a pace that works for him. And this is all influenced by the individual dog, the particular behavior you are teaching, the reward you are using, and, in the end, your skill.

I strongly suggest enrolling in a class with a competent trainer versed not only in nonviolent training principles, but also in the correct use of reinforcement schedules. Hopefully you will find a trainer who is able to make these principles understandable to you. It's like learning to play a musical instrument. You can learn to read music from a book, but until you hear it played by a professional, you really don't know how it's supposed to sound. Also, visual learners, like myself, need to see someone in action in order to understand or "grok" it and then polish their skills. For that reason, I also suggest the videos listed in Appendix D. The following books are also helpful if you want to pursue a deeper study of the use of reinforcement schedules: *The Culture Clash* by Jean Donaldson, *Clicker Training for Obedience* by Morgan Spector, *Excel-erated Learning* by Dr. Pam Reid, and *Don't Shoot the Dog* by Karen Pryor.

Remember, timing is everything in dog training. Seeing a qualified professional apply these principles skillfully is worth its weight in squeaky toys!

Markers—Clickers, Whistles, and Words

Dogs have only a short window of time in which they associate what they're doing with a consequence—whether it is a reward or a punishment. Let's say you are teaching your dog to sit. When your dog puts his behind on the floor you've got up to *one second* to let him know, "That's it. That's the behavior I'm looking for!" In other words, in order to get the message across to him, you have to give him your signal of approval virtually the exact moment he sits. If you walk into a room three seconds after your dog has eliminated on the carpet, there's no use even commenting on it. Your dog simply won't associate his urination three seconds before with your yelling. As far as he's concerned, you're yelling because of what he's doing at that exact moment—lying quietly on the floor. (See more on how to deal with elimination problems on page 207.)

So how can you develop the split-second speed required to communicate how pleased you are with your dog for sitting when you ask him to? How do we get information to our dogs so quickly? It can be pretty difficult to consistently deliver a food treat in a split second to reward your dog every time you see a behavior you're looking for. So do what the famous behaviorist Pavlov did—turn a sound into a reward. After all, it's far easier to deliver a "sound" reward than it is to deliver a piece of food. And it's possible to make a sound as good as a food reward in your dog's eyes.

The tool we use to give this sound reward is a clicker. A clicker is a cricket-sounding toy used by many dog trainers to clearly and crisply mark a dog's behavior. Your dog learns to work for the click just as he does when he is motivated by food. These inexpensive tools are small plastic boxes about the size of a matchbox. A clicker gives your dog information very fast. Remember, you need to reward your dog virtually the same moment she's doing it in order to let her know she has performed the desired behavior. Normally our ability to respond verbally is simply not that fast or consistent—that's why we use a click to mark the behavior. A clicker is a quick, accurate, novel tool that can mark your dog's behavior as good, something you want her to do again.

In his book *Clicker Training for Obedience,* Morgan Spector explains: "So, *it is a rule* that every time you click you are signaling to the dog that he has done what you want, and the behavior is over. And so, it is a rule also that when you click, the dog is free to stop what he is doing and get his treat."[1] Eventually you'll stop using the clicker and just use the word "okay" or "free" to signify the end of the exercise and release the dog. (Clickers are difficult to find in stores, but they can be ordered by calling 1-800-269-3591 or on the internet at www.raisewithpraise.com.)

How to Use a Clicker
Initially a clicker has no value to your dog. It's neutral. To give it value or empower it, do this: Put it in your hand and *immediately* after clicking, throw your dog a great food treat. Click and treat like this ten to fifteen times. Do two or three of these sessions during the day. You'll know your dog has "got it" when she starts looking around for the treat after hearing the click. Now that the clicker has meaning, you're ready to "mark" the exact behavior you're looking for. For example, when teaching your dog to sit, move your hand an inch or so over her head. If she sits, click and reward the moment her behind hits the floor.

Note: Some dogs are a bit sound sensitive, so be cautious and sensitive when introducing the clicker.

---

[1] Spector, Morgan, *Clicker Training for Obedience,* Sunshine Books, 1999, page 13.

Notes on Using a Clicker

If your dog is shy or sensitive to sounds, it helps to do a little planning when introducing the use of a clicker. Here are some tips:

- Make sure you use your dog's absolute favorite food as a treat in conjunction with the use of the clicker.
- Muffle the clicker by putting it in your pocket or wrapping a towel around it and increase your distance from your dog.
- Instead of doing a complete click, which consists of two clicking sounds—one when you press the clicker and another when you release it—press for one click only. Then, the next time your dog does a desired behavior, release your thumb to make another clicking sound.
- As soon as you click, throw the treat or have someone who is standing next to your dog immediately drop the treat.
- Single click and treat three to five times and then stop. Remember, the treat is given a split second *after* the click. Repeat the process later.
- Make sure your demeanor is happy and fun.
- Gradually close the distance to your dog. For especially sensitive dogs this may take a couple of days.
- Once your dog associates the muffled single click with the treat, you can try a muffled double click. Then graduate to an unmuffled double click.

Trainers at marine mammal water parks use whistles as "markers" instead of clickers when they train whales and dolphins. A clicker doesn't work for them because they need their hands free to give two-handed signals. Although a whistle can work in training your dog, I prefer a clicker because when you use a whistle, you can't simultaneously give verbal praise to your dog.

Deaf people use flashes of light from a flashlight, a laser pen-light, or a light in the room as markers. They also use other methods to mark a behavior, such as touching the dog or giving a hand signal.

If you don't yet have a clicker, you can use words to mark a desired behavior. For instance, say "good dog" every time your dog sits and he'll get the idea. However, clickers work much better than word markers because:

1. they're different and novel for both human and dog,
2. they're much quicker because it's difficult to say the word "good" as fast as you can click, and
3. a clicker can be used as an "occasion setter."

An occasion setter is any stimulus that triggers a dog's anticipation that something good or bad is going to happen. For instance, when you open a can of food, he anticipates that he is going to eat. When you grab the leash, he anticipates going for a walk. Just like these examples of positive anticipation, when you grab the clicker it can mean that fun times are ahead. It's as if you flip on a switch in your dog's head and he's suddenly ready to work. He'll immediately recognize the clicker and say to himself, "Oh boy, something good is about to happen." This is an important concept because no dog is "on" all the time. An occasion setter can flip on a switch in your dog's head that helps him tune in to you and pay attention.

Remember to click immediately when your dog does the desired behavior and reward with a treat. Otherwise, he won't associate the click and treat with the behavior.

"No-Reward" Markers

Dog expert Gary Wilkes popularized a training tool called the no-reward marker. Just as a clicker, whistle, or the word "good" can mark a correct response, you can help your dog learn by letting him know when he makes an incorrect response. You do this by using a no-reward marker such as the word "oops," "ah-ah," or "uh-oh." Let's say you ask your dog to sit. You give her two seconds. If she doesn't sit, say "oops" and remove the chance of getting a reward. Another example is asking her to stay. If she gets up right away, say "oops" and turn away.

Two things are happening here:

1. If your dog doesn't do what you've asked, you've gone too far too fast. So you have to go back to the point where she was successful and build from there; but . . .
2. She's also learned that she's really in control of getting a reward because you've identified not only what behavior gets her the reward—the sound of the clicker—she's also learned what not to do by your signal of "oops."

Targeting

Any object or a sound can be used as a target, which is something a dog is taught to focus on and interact with. Here are two examples: Let's say we're at a wedding reception. If I asked you to go stand by the cake for a picture, the cake would be a target—an object related to a specific location. Or, did you ever watch television and see the host look at the floor for his mark? It's usually an "X" made of tape that designates where he's supposed to stand for the cameras. That's his target.

As you'll learn in the lessons in Part II of this book, for some behaviors you will begin by teaching your dog to touch your hand with his nose. In that case, your hand is the target. Similarly, instead of using your hand as a target, you can teach a dog to touch a stick, toy, light switch, or almost anything else with his nose or paw. At the marine mammal water parks, targets include balls and other toys, large posters of various shapes and sizes, and all sorts of other objects.

By teaching animals to touch a target—whether with a paw or other body part—you can get them to do all kinds of stuff. Let's say you teach your dog to target your index finger or your left hand. If you put your hand down by your side and tell your dog to touch it with her nose, what have you got? Well, once you start walking, your dog is now "heeling." If you teach a dog to paw a light switch as the target, you've got a dog who can now turn the lights off. Teach this same dog to flip the switch upward with his nose and he can then turn the lights on. If you're using a target stick or a point of light from a laser pen (see Target Sticks on page 125), you can teach your dog to sit, lie down, go through a doggie tunnel, climb ladders, and open doors.

Targeting is a wonderful way to entice or lure your dog and get her to go where you want her to go, joyfully doing what you want her to do. For more in-depth study on targeting, I suggest the videos by Gary Wilkes and Karen Pryor. Also, the book *Clicker Training for Obedience Competition*, by Morgan Spector includes a section on targeting. (See Appendix C for suppliers.)

(Also see Targets and Target Sticks on page 125 of Chapter 8.)

chapter seven

The 8 Tools of Dog Training

Nonviolent, reward-based dog training means taking the path of least resistance. Imagine a clean, sweet river, fed from the Rocky Mountains and gently drifting all the way to the Gulf of Mexico. Steering a canoe down that river is much easier than trying to swim upstream. Harvesting the river's energy is easier than trying to stop its flow. Before every formal training session, think of this flow. The river moves around boulders that are in its way. Likewise, obstacles represented by your dog's internal and external distractions don't have to be eliminated; you can go around them and even work with them. The way to do this is to keep your focus. Keep your mind on the goal while remaining flexible, adjusting the specific training methods and the training environment you are using for any given situation or moment of time.

The birth of modern, user-friendly, dog-friendly training began with the methods used in the training of military dogs by British Army officer Colonel E. H. Richardson during the First World War. However, the introduction to the masses of what is now recognized as scientific dog training came with the work of Karen Pryor, a former head trainer at Hawaii's Sea Life Park. In her work with marine mammals, Pryor found that positive reinforcement was a powerful tool in training killer whales, dolphins, and other sea animals. In 1986, she introduced these scientific behavioral principles in her book *Don't Shoot the Dog*, which presents tools for training your dog as well as ways in which these principles work for other animals, including humans. In her book Pryor not only shows you how to shape your dog's behavior without strain or pain, she also shares how to combat your own addictions to alcohol, drugs, cigarettes, and overeating; how to deal with problems such as a moody spouse, an impossible teen, or an aged parent; and even how to improve your tennis game.

With the following eight tools, as presented in *Don't Shoot the Dog*, Pryor helped the layperson understand why people and animals do what they do. These eight tools were later adapted by others, including Terry Ryan, who wrote the excellent book, *The Toolbox for Remodeling Problem Behavior*. I have also restructured Pryor's eight tools to some extent, in order to align these concepts with my own style.

These tools represent the eight different ways you can modify your dog's behavior; that is, get what you *want* from your dog and eliminate what you *don't want*. From this perspective and from the dog's point of view, there is really no such thing as a problem behavior. Most behaviors that are problems for humans can be resolved by using one of these tools or a combination of several of them. When you begin to work with them, they will soon make total sense to you and using them will eventually become second nature.

Note: Health problems can lead to problems in training. Before beginning your training program, have your dog's health checked by your veterinarian.

1. *Withdraw the reward and ignore the undesirable behavior:* Also known as *extinction*, this training tool goes back to the principle that a dog stops what he's doing if he doesn't get "paid" in some way, shape, or form. In other words, when there is no longer a reward attached to a certain behavior, the behavior generally ceases. In psychology this is known as extinction. You can think of it as extinguishing a fire; after all, if you don't feed a fire, it goes out. Think about what your dog gets out of the barking, jumping, chewing, digging, begging, etc. How is he being rewarded for the behavior? Dogs are, after all, pretty

smart. In many cases, the dog's reward for the undesirable behavior is your attention. When you withdraw your attention, the undesirable behavior usually stops. If you stop giving your dog attention for barking, he has no incentive to continue. If you stop giving treats when he begs at the table, there's a good chance he'll eventually stop because there's simply no longer any reason to continue.

Jumping is another great example of how well ignoring a behavior works. Dogs generally get attention when they jump. Sometimes the attention comes in the form of being petted; other times they get yelled at. When you stop petting and stop yelling, the jumping usually stops. There are cases, however, in which withdrawing the reward and ignoring the undesirable behavior results in the dog resorting to another type of undesirable behavior. For instance, when he stops begging for treats at the table, he may try something else—like barking. When this happens, you have to go through the process again; this time ignoring the barking. This training tool works well when combined with tool number 2, positive reinforcement.

2. *Positive reinforcement*: This is an easy one. The second tool of dog training is positive reinforcement. As with the example in Chapter 1, if I give you $10,000 for sitting in a chair, you're pretty likely to sit there again. Figure out what your dog likes— praise, social freedom, food, toys—and use these rewards to reinforce the behaviors you want.

3. *Deliver a "negative"*: As I've said many times, the philosophy behind my training method doesn't include jerking, hitting, kicking, shocking, shaking, ear pinching, or yelling. So what could be left that's considered a negative? In the step-by-step lessons in Part II of this book, you'll learn the magnet game. (See page 159.) In this game, when the dog does something you like, you approach and pet him or throw him a treat. The dog's behavior acts like a magnet that draws you—and other rewards—closer. Imagine this: You're on the couch watching *Touched by an Angel* and you notice your dog lying down. In this case, lying down is the magnetic behavior. You get up to pet

him. But when you are halfway there, he gets up. Since the behavior you want to reward is lying down, you stop in your tracks, turn around, and head back to the couch. Seeing you go the other way is a negative to your dog because he wants to be with you. He will very quickly learn that staying in the down position will bring you close.

Here's another example: My dog Molly used to bark at strangers while she sat in the car waiting for me to return. In order to change this behavior, I engaged the help of a friend who was a stranger to Molly. We walked toward the car together and, as Molly began to bark, the stranger and I both stopped in our tracks and backed up. She would bark and we'd back up. She'd be quiet and we would approach. Then she'd bark again and we'd back up farther. Now she was confused. She wanted the stranger to go away but she wanted me to approach. I used the tool of *positive reinforcement* (tool number 2). When she stopped barking, we moved forward and I praised her, which was her reward. When she started to bark again, we used tool number 3 and *delivered a negative*, we immediately backed away again. After several repetitions of this lesson, Molly got the point. She learned that when she was quiet she would be rewarded and when she barked, her rewards would be removed. As a result, she stopped barking while waiting in the car for me. This is a classic example of the magnet game, which is taught on page 159.

If chewing is a problem, you can deliver another type of negative such as putting something that tastes bad on the leash or other object. Bitter apple is a liquid that tastes, well, bitter. It usually works. If it doesn't work, try Listerine mouthwash. If that doesn't work you may have to resort to bitter orange, which must be prescribed by your veterinarian. There are many other products you can use as negatives, but stay away from things that burn like Tabasco and hot chilies.

4. *Remove the cause of the behavior*: This training tool is also called the causative approach. Determine what is causing the behavior and then simply remove it from the dog's environment. For example, if your dog is barking at another dog, block

his view or take the other dog away. Another obvious example is this: if your dog is experiencing pain from a burr in his behind, he may not be willing to sit. If you remove the burr, he'll sit again. Or, remove the noisy vacuum cleaner and he'll stop urinating. Remove the boredom and replace it with exercise, training and smart toys (see page 34) and he'll stop barking, chewing up the furniture, and destroying the house.

5. *Substitute another behavior*: With substitution, you simply substitute a desirable behavior for an undesirable one. Instead of asking, "How do I stop my dog from doing such and such?" start asking, "What do I *want* my dog to do in this situation?" For instance, instead of "How do I get my dog to stop jumping on me when I walk in the door?" ask yourself, "What do I want my dog to do to get my attention and affection when I come home?" One way to do this would be to teach her to sit or lie down when you walk in the door and then spend a minute or two giving attention and affection by praising her, scratching her behind the ears, and so on. Another example of substitution is to throw a tennis ball to a barking dog and teach him to hold it in his mouth (retrieve). Once he's got the tennis ball in his mouth, he can't bark. (Well, he can still make noise—but he won't be able to bark.) When you use the tool of substitution, you are diverting your dog's attention and asking him to do another behavior that is incompatible with or replaces the behavior that is unacceptable.

6. *Change the association with the object from an undesirable behavior to a positive one*: With this tool, which is also called counter-conditioning, you are changing the association or how your dog perceives the situation. For instance, if your dog barks at the mail carrier, the next-door neighbor with a beard, or the vacuum cleaner, it's obvious that, for whatever reason, she's not too comfortable with that person or object. Other dislikes might include hair dryers, nail clippers, and police sirens. Counter-conditioning means teaching your dog to look at these things as positive. This method takes time but works really well with many problem behaviors. Just as soon as the mail carrier shows up, distract your dog with sound and/or motion, then ask him to

sit and give him a $10,000 treat. Do the same thing over and over again—associate the mail carrier with a great treat. Eventually, you can enroll the mail carrier in your effort, asking him to come closer and closer to the dog on each visit. Finally, he can give the dog a treat himself. As for clippers, vacuums, and so on, you can combine counter-conditioning with tool number 7, *put the behavior on cue*.

Dog expert William E. Campbell developed what he called the Jolly Routine to change the dog's association with an object from a negative to a positive. In his book *Better Behavior in Dogs,* Campbell presents it this way:

The Jolly Routine

Make arrangements so you can create the noises or situations that cause the dog's fearful behavior. Also, be prepared to produce a situation that makes your dog wag his tail and act happy. Each dog has his favorite toy or some key word that causes him to act happy. If yours does not have one, you will need to create one. Try bouncing a ball, playing with a toy, laughing— anything that causes a wagging, happy response; even rattling car keys can work.

After this groundwork is laid, produce the situation that causes the fear behavior. But, the instant you do so, produce the happy-type stimulus—the Jolly Routine—with gusto! It is marvelously effective when carried out with conviction. Don't wait for the dog to get fearful. Introduce the jolly element immediately. Not even a half-second should elapse between the fear stimulus and happy elements.

When you apply the Jolly Routine, here is what should happen: At first your dog may appear a little confused and may even fall into his fear pattern. Even so, keep up the Jolly Routine for a minute or two, then go on about some other business. Pay no further atten-tion to the dog. After about five minutes, repeat the whole process. Do this no more than four times, twice a day if possible. Allow at least three hours between any two, complete Jolly Routine exercise setups. You will know you are succeeding when you see the dog begin to wag his tail even before you start the jolly business. Continue the process for six weeks. If you see any backsliding, merely restart the program.[1]

7. *Put the behavior on cue:* If you're dealing with a problem behavior, this particular tool of dog training is a bit like reverse psychology. Let's say your dog is barking at virtually everything that exists: doorbells, people who move quickly, other dogs barking or coming into the yard, the phone, and so on. When you *put the desired behavior on cue*, you are telling the dog that barking is the exact behavior you're looking for. (Review how to use a clicker on page 105.) When the dog barks, click and reward the barking. Then encourage her to bark again. Click and reward. Associate a word and/or a hand signal with the barking and use it whenever your dog barks. I use the word "sing" and move my hands like I'm conducting an orchestra. Within no time, your dog will start barking on cue. The next step is to reward the silence. Say "quiet" in a voice that is startling but not scary. (You're trying to interrupt the dog, not frighten her.) As soon as she quiets down, click and reward. Now you've got barking when you ask and quiet when you ask. Nifty, huh!

8. *Get your dog used to it:* In some situations, the only way to get your dog to accept a person, animal, or object he objects to, such as the mail carrier, the neighbor's dog, or a vacuum cleaner, is to get him used to it. There are three ways to get a dog used to something:

   A. Systematic desensitization: Introduce the scary person, animal, or object *a little at a time* and then over a gradually extended period of time present the sight, sound, or touch of this person, animal, or object over and over again. Gradually increase the intensity of the person, animal, or

---

[1] Campbell, William E., *The New Better Behavior in Dogs: A Guide to Solving All Your Dog's Problems,* Alpine Publications, Inc., 1999, page 196.

object. For an object like a bell, this is done by ringing it softly, then louder and louder. With an animal or person, start at a comfortable distance and slowly bring the animal or person closer and closer. For example, if your dog barks at another dog, start training at a distance far enough away from the other dog that your dog will no longer be distracted and will pay more attention to you. Then gradually bring the dogs closer together. Repeat this gradual process until the second dog no longer represents a threat to your dog. Desensitization can be used with a dog that is afraid of firecrackers, thunderstorms, and other loud noises, or that is sensitive to movement, like a person getting out of a chair quickly. This method also works hand-in-hand with positive reinforcement (tool number 2).

B. Habituation: If your dog doesn't like the sound of the doorbell, continue ringing it over and over until your dog gets bored with the sound. In other words, it will become "ho-hum" because it is no longer relevant.

C. Flooding: With this method, you *flood* the dog with the sights, sounds, and touches of the person, animal, or object that causes him problems. For instance, if he doesn't like other people, take him into a crowded room.

Of all of the eight tools of dog training, this one is the trickiest since it can be difficult to know which of these three methods is preferable. You may have to consult a professional dog trainer to know which one is best for your dog's unique situation. If you do the wrong thing, you could make matters worse. Obviously, all of these methods must be used with compassion, skill, and understanding.

The suggestions offered in this section are examples for shaping general behaviors. Part III of this book deals with problem behaviors in more detail.

So, how to do you know which of the eight tools to use to handle a problem behavior? Here's a bird's-eye view of the process to determine the best tool.

Behavioral Building Blocks

The following chart will help you determine how to deal with a "problem" behavior. For illustration purposes, I'm using barking as an example.

A **When and where does the barking happen?**
When the doorbell rings or other sounds occur?
When my dog looks out the window and sees people or animals?
When my dog is at the door?
When I'm on the phone?
When I'm in the kitchen?
When my dog is in the car?
When certain people are around?
In the morning? Afternoon? Evening?
Other?

B **Review each of the 9 ingredients and select the ones that contribute to your dog's "problem" behavior.**
The examples that follow are just a sampling of the ways an imbalance in the 9 ingredients can impact training. (See Chapter 2 to review the 9 ingredients.)

Food: Is your dog stressed because she's hungry or is she suffering from indigestion or a food allergy?
Play: Is your dog bored and understimulated?
Socialization: Does your dog get to mingle with other dogs, other animals, and other humans, and is he given a chance to adapt to the sights, sounds, smells, and touches of his environment?
Quiet Time: Is your dog given time to get away from it all or is he dis-stressed and over his stress management threshold?

Exercise: Does your dog get a chance to run and express his energy? Are his muscles weak or tight? Is he in pain?

Employment: Does your dog have a job to do? Has he lost confidence because he doesn't know what is expected of him?

Rest: Is your dog exhausted? Does he just want to be left alone?

Training: Is your dog confused because he was never taught what to do? Is he in a learning dip? Have you unintentionally trained him to do the "problem" behavior? (Also see Unintentional Training on page 201.)

Health Care: Have you checked for allergies or physical problems such as a thorn in the paw, parasites, matted hair, fleas, arthritis, etc.? Is your dog too young or too old to do what you are asking of him?

C Set your goal. What behavior do you want from your dog?

Bark 3 times and then stop.
Bark only when asked and ignore everything else.
Bark only at people who are carrying monkeys on their backs.
Other.

D Select one or more of the 8 tools of training to change your dog's behavior

Withdraw the reward and ignore the undesirable behavior
Positive reinforcement
Deliver a "negative"
Remove the cause of the behavior
Substitute another behavior
Change the association with the object from an undesirable behavior to a positive one
Put the behavior on cue
Get your dog used to it

chapter eight

Training Gear: Collars, Leashes, Clickers, Target Sticks, and Kennels

Certain training equipment can really help create an optimum learning environment—an environment that promotes safety, fun, and the driving motivation to learn.

Collars

In nonviolent training, the commonly used *choke collars*, also referred to as *training collars* or *slip collars*, are not acceptable because of the potential for hurting the dog, especially while you are developing the skill to use them correctly. While the methods I teach involve no jerking at all on the leash and collar, it's important that I clarify here that it is possible for some professional trainers to give a gentle tug on the leash and collar to get information to the dog without inflicting any harm. I know several trainers who have the skill, touch, and timing necessary to use the leash and collar nonviolently in this way. But to get to that level of proficiency takes time and practice and necessitates learning to "read" each individual dog in order to know how much or how little intensity to use. Too much intensity and the dog can be injured; too little and the method proves ineffective. And timing is critical—too soon and the dog gets confused; too late and the dog gets confused.

A simple tug on the leash can and does easily get out of hand and is harmful to the dog. Most people immediately fall into a trap and feel that if a little "attention grabbing" jerk on the leash is successful—well, then a more serious pop will just hurry things along that much quicker. In the process, the dog acts as a guinea pig and could sustain injury. The line between a slight "pop" on the leash to get attention and a stronger "pop" that inflicts discomfort or pain can be difficult for most people to determine. The bottom line is that it is not necessary to use any jerking at all to get your dog to do what you want.

Prong and *shock collars* (also referred to as *electronic collars*) are unacceptable for the same reasons as choke collars. Prong collars look like medieval torture devices, while shock collars actually deliver an electric shock. Both of these types of collars are designed to deliver pain or discomfort, especially when the dog pulls on the leash. Many popular training systems actually tell you to use a shock collar and "set the degree of correction you want" to correct your dog when he is doing something you don't want him to do. Other, supposedly more gentle training methods promote the use of these collars to "get your dog's attention"; the rationale is that prongs and electric shocks don't inflict pain. However, the difference between a "static electricity charge similar to walking across a carpet" and a jolt that kicks the eyeballs loose can be blurry.

ILLUSTRATION 9A

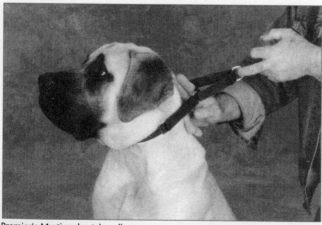

Premier's Martingale-style collar.

ILLUSTRATION 9B

Gentle Leader halter-style collar.

ILLUSTRATION 9C

So what type of collars should you use? For a smaller dog, I suggest a body harness collar that fits around the front half of the body. For medium to large dogs, one type of Martingale-style collar, such as the one from Premier Pet Products, is preferable because it never closes completely around the dog's neck. These collars are ingeniously designed so they can never choke a dog.

If you have a problem with a dog that pulls on the leash, try a halter-style collar (also called a nose harness collar). My favorite type of halter-style collar is called the Gentle Leader, which is also made by Premier, though several similar styles are sold at major pet stores. These collars work on the premise that where the head goes, the body follows. Most dogs get used to these collars without problems, although on rare occasions a dog just doesn't seem to adjust to it. One problem that can develop with the halter-style collar is the way people use it. When the dog pulls on the leash to greet another dog and the handler doesn't allow enough slack, the dog is unable to use his doggie communication body language with the other dog. If you hold the dog's head up, for example, he can't go through the dog greeting ritual, which sometimes involves looking away, sniffing the ground, or turning his side to the other dog. You must remember to keep the leash slack to avoid these problems.

Another problem with the halter-type collar is a public relations problem because some people mistake them for muzzles. Hence, strangers perceive a dog wearing this collar as dangerous. Unlike muzzles, dogs *can* bark, eat, and drink, and even bite with halter-style collars on. However, you might find yourself repeatedly telling people, "Don't worry, this isn't a muzzle. He doesn't bite." This problem can be somewhat ameliorated by choosing a collar that blends with the color of the dog's coat or a brightly colored one that makes people think the collar is fun and nonthreatening.

Leashes

When used properly as a management tool, the leash is a vital part of a safe training environment. For everyday purposes, choose a leash that is 4 to 6 feet long and made of nylon. For distance training work, you'll also need a 20-foot leash and you might even want a 50-foot leash. I prefer nylon because it's light and flexible. Stay away from chain leashes because they are too heavy and get caught on things.

William Campbell, a renowned behaviorist from Oregon, has developed a leash called Sof-Touch™, which has an ingenious design. A piece of elastic that is built into the leash helps to further reduce the possibility of a dog hurting himself if he happens to bolt away from you. As the dog pulls, he feels an extra bit of tension on the leash and has a split second to stop before running out of leash. This leash can help prevent the risk of spinal injury.

When you tether your dog at night, don't use a nylon leash. For one thing, some dogs chew right through them. Also, a nylon leash can get wrapped around the dog's leg, neck, or body and cause an injury. So instead of a regular leash, use a tether made of wire cable like the ones used to attach a bicycle to a bicycle rack. This wire cable is stiff so the dog can't chew through it or get wrapped up in it. It should be just long enough for the dog to move around—approximately 2 1/2 feet, depending on the size of your dog, of course. (Also see Managing Your Dog on page 133 for instructions on how to properly tether your dog.)

Clickers

As described in Chapter 6, the clicker can be a valuable training tool. Clickers are almost impossible to find in stores, but can be purchased by calling 1-800-269-3591 or on the internet at www.raisewithpraise.com.

Targets and Target Sticks

One of the quickest ways to teach a dog to do a specific behavior is to use a target or target stick. (Review the section on targeting in Chapter 6, page 108). A target can be almost anything—including your finger; any wooden, metal, or plastic stick; a laser light; a ball; or a piece of colored paper. The target sticks used in my classes are simple wooden dowels that are about 1/4 inch in diameter and 3 feet long. You can buy one in any lumber, hardware, or building supply store. Color about 1 inch of one end with a red marker as the specific target.

Fancier target sticks that fold into two or three sections are also available. They can be purchased from Direct Book Service (see Appendix C). Since it's easier to understand how a target stick is used in training when you see it, I also suggest attending a class on this subject or purchasing a video (see Appendix D).

Kennels

A portable kennel is an important training tool for managing your dog safely. Along with the proper use of leashes and baby gates, use of the kennel helps to keep your dog, your family, and the environment out of harm's way. Getting your dog to absolutely love going to the kennel— her "safe spot"—is your first priority. (See Go to Your Spot in the lessons in Part II on page 170.) Kennels, like anything else, are as helpful and useful or as cruel and negative as we make them. I love the use of kennels as long as you take the time to introduce your dog to it in a positive way.

Your dog should be taught on a gradual schedule to love spending time in her kennel, so she views it as "home, sweet home." With correct use, most puppies get used to the kennel very quickly. For an older dog or puppies that are having problems adapting to the kennel, don't use it until the dog has formed a positive association with it. Instead, put the dog in the kitchen behind a baby gate or a dog pen, which is like a kennel without a top, similar to a baby's playpen. Your other option, of course, is to tether your dog with a leash at night.

Put the kennel in your bedroom. It will help greatly with the socialization process. Your dog should not be expected to spend more than four hours in the kennel at any one stretch of time, unless it's at night when seven hours is maximum. (See Eliminating on page 207 to be sure you aren't expecting your puppy to "hold it" too long.)

Please be sure to take your dog's collar off before putting her in the kennel. Hard as it is to believe, I've known of dogs that have gotten the collar caught on something, causing them to almost choke to death. And do not leave rubber toys or rawhide chews in the kennel; I know of several dogs that have choked on them also.

Kennels come in two basic models. Some are open, like the wire-cage models, and others have solid walls, with wire only at the gate, like the airline travel models. Whichever type you choose, pick one that allows your dog to stand without stooping and lie down without curling her body. If you are buying a kennel for a puppy, be sure to get one that will be large enough for her when she's fully grown. If your dog is a pure breed, it's not too difficult to determine how large she will be as an adult. However, if your dog is a mixed breed, ask your veterinarian approximately how much your dog will grow before picking a kennel. While she's a puppy, you can block off part of the interior of the kennel so she doesn't have room to eliminate in it. As she gets bigger, simply remove the barrier.

Remember, the kennel is an item you will be keeping for years and years. It is your dog's "safe spot." It's worth it to spend a little more for a quality kennel that will last. There are some less expensive models on the market that can present problems. For instance, I've known dogs to catch a nail or get cut on the wires of the kennel or even get their head stuck. (See Appendix C for mail-order distributors.)

Beds

I also suggest purchasing a bed for your dog. This can range from a simple mat to an embroidered, plush cushion complete with your dog's name. Once again, it can be used as your dog's safe spot and can be a wonderful security object.

chapter nine

Safety for Your Dog and Family

Preventing Dog Bites

Over four million people suffer from dog bites every year in the United States alone. If this statistic isn't bad enough, over two million of them are children. In fact, more children suffer from dog bites every year than from the combined annual totals for measles, mumps, chicken pox, and whooping cough. Children who are ages five to nine are the primary victims of animal bites. Seventy-five percent of these bites are from dogs that the victim knows. Injuries to the head, neck, and face are common in young children. These injuries often cause significant trauma and many require hospitalization.

Education is the key to preventing dog bites. The risk of a bite can be reduced dramatically when children and adults are taught how to approach and handle dogs, read the warning signals, and avoid risky situations. In our society, we teach children how to telephone for emergency help, cross the street safely, and avoid threatening situations with strangers. It's just as important to teach them how to respect a dog and understand her needs, without instilling fear. In my *Nonviolence Works!* programs in elementary schools, I do just that.

Here are the safety rules I share with kids. Of course, they work for adults, too.

1. *Always* ask permission before approaching or petting a dog. This is especially important for children.
2. Don't pet or approach an unfamiliar dog, especially if food or toys are involved.
3. Don't approach or pet a strange, untrained, or injured dog. Also, don't approach a strange dog if the dog's exit is blocked or if the dog is up against a wall.
4. Stay out of other people's yards.
5. Never tease a dog.
6. Don't blow puffs of air into a dog's face, pull a dog's tail, or try to lift a dog off the ground.
7. Don't wake a sleeping dog.
8. Instruct children never to run through the house waving their arms. This can excite some dogs who then want to join in the fun and chase the children, which could lead to an accident.

(Also see Dog Etiquette—How to Greet a Dog on page 77.)

Keeping Your Dog Safe

You can "puppy proof" the environment to prevent or at least minimize the potential for accidents by removing or locking up chewable and toxic objects. Of course, there's no substitute for good old common sense when it comes to preventing accidents.

Items to Keep Out of Your Dog's Reach

- *Chocolate*: Though you may think you're giving your dog a nice treat, avoid giving chocolate or leaving it out where your dog could snatch it. A component of chocolate is toxic to dogs and can even cause death.
- *Plants*: There's a long list of plants that are toxic to dogs. They include poinsettias, ferns, mistletoe, philodendrons, spider

plants, oleander, and a host of others. Check with your veterinarian about other toxic plants.

Medicines and household cleaners: Protect your dog from these items by keeping your cabinets locked. A small prescription bottle could seem like a fun toy that rattles; then, if your dog cracks it open, the medication inside could be extremely harmful to him.

Household and office items: Plastic bags, plastic ties, balloons, rubber bands, tinsel, string, paper clips, needles, pens, pencils, and any sharp object could be dangerous if your dog bites it or ingests it.

Food or leftovers such as cooked chicken and turkey bones. Your dog could choke on a bone if he gets into the trash. Practice management by putting him in a kennel so he can't get to "illegal" objects or practice prevention by putting the kitchen wastebasket in a safe place where he can't get to it.

Children's toys: Some toys can be dangerous, particularly if a dog could tear or chew off a part and choke on it. Instead of leaving children's toys out, use smart doggie toys like Kongs, Pedigree plastic balls, or Buster Cubes.

Electric wires and cords: A puppy or dog could be injured if he chews on a wire or cord.

Tablecloths: A puppy could pull on an overhanging tablecloth and be injured by a falling object.

Antifreeze: Dogs find the taste of antifreeze appealing. Unfortunately, it can be deadly. *If your dog ingests even a small amount of antifreeze, call your veterinarian immediately.* A safer type of antifreeze is available; ask your veterinarian about this.

Rat poison: This is another toxic and deadly substance that dogs have been known to ingest. *If you suspect your dog has ingested rat poison, call your veterinarian immediately.*

Toilet bowl cleaners: Don't use a toilet bowl cleaner that is placed in the tank. The toxic chemicals can cause illness if your dog should happen to drink from the toilet.

There are several other ways you can be proactive to keep your dog both safe and healthy.

Ways to Keep Your Dog Healthy

🦴 *Prevent heatstroke: Never* leave your dog in a car in warm weather. Every year news reports abound with cases of both infants and dogs that were left in a car in hot weather with disastrous results. The popular idea of cracking a window so she'll get some air is fine if the temperature isn't too high and you're parked in the shade, but it really doesn't help at all when it's hot outside and the sun bakes down on a parked car. Also, remember that the sun moves—one minute your car might be parked in the shade and a few minutes later it might be in direct sunlight. If the temperature is 85 degrees Fahrenheit outside on a hot summer day, the inside of the car can reach 160 degrees Fahrenheit within half an hour. Your dog can suffer brain damage or death if her body temperature reaches 107 degrees Fahrenheit, which is only five degrees over her normal body temperature. Signs of heatstroke include: excessive panting, vomiting, a fast pulse rate, and high body temperature. If you suspect heatstroke, do not delay. Get your dog to a veterinarian immediately. If that's not possible, soak your dog in cool water until her temperature goes down. Ice packs around your dog's head will also help.

Don't take your dog along with you in hot weather if you're going to have to leave her in the car for even a few minutes. In those emergency situations when you have to take your dog with you in hot weather, I suggest leaving the air conditioning running. Another option is to make a bed of ice for the dog to lie on. You can do this by filling a large plastic tray with ice and covering it with a towel. But even in these situations, the bottom line is this—never stay away for more than a few minutes. In Florida and Michigan, it's actually illegal to leave your dog alone in the car.

🦴 *Vaccinate for contagious diseases:* Puppies can pick up a parvovirus from any area that an infected dog has visited. Therefore, until your dog has had a full round of parvovirus vaccinations and is at least sixteen weeks old, carry him when you are in unfamiliar environments. There is some controversy among holistic veterinarians as to which other vaccinations should be given; however, I feel vaccinations for rabies, distemper, and heartworm are vital. Additionally, some boarding kennels require that dogs be vaccinated for kennel cough.

Managing Your Dog

It is important to physically control your dog until she learns what to do and what not to do. Use of a leash and collar, as well as a kennel, will help immensely in this process. Introduce these items to your dog using positive reinforcement. There is no need to use the kennel as a punishment. Leash management includes tethering your dog to the bottom of furniture, to you by hooking the leash to your belt or around your waist, or to a doorknob. To hook a leash to a doorknob, open the door and slip the leash handle over the door handle on the other side. Drop the leash to the floor and slip it under the door. Close the door. The idea is to keep the leash flat along the floor so your dog won't choke herself or get tangled up in the leash.

ILLUSTRATION 10

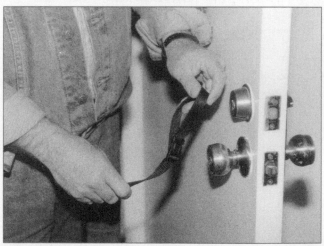

The safest way to tether your dog to a door: Slip the leash handle over the doorknob on the other side of the door, drop the leash to the floor and slip it under the door. Then close the door. *Never tether your dog unless you are there to supervise.*

ILLUSTRATION 11

ILLUSTRATION 12

Never tether a dog while she's left alone.

Always use leash management to keep your dog from running to the street and be respectful by keeping him off other peoples' yards. Since some lawns are chemically treated, you don't want your dog to be exposed to these chemicals.

Watch for broken glass on sidewalks. In hot weather, be aware of the temperature of the pavement. If it's too hot, your dog's paws could be burned. And be aware that your dog can get sunburned too, so take necessary precautions and avoid taking her outside during the hottest hours of the day. In the winter, salt that is used to melt snow and ice can also be a problem. You don't want her to ingest too much sodium when she licks her paws, so be sure to wipe her paws when you bring her inside.

Don't allow your dog to ride loose in the back of your pick-up truck. This seems like a commonsense notion, but I've actually witnessed a dog being flipped out of a truck and others holding on for dear life. I also suggest seat belts when your dog is in the car. If they're good enough for us, they're good enough for our dogs. Don't allow your dog to hang his head out the window. This can be dangerous for a couple of reasons—stones can be thrown from the pavement by passing cars and cut your dog's head or eyes, and insects can get in the eyes.

PART II

The Lessons

The Learning Baseline

Whenever you ask your dog to do something, it makes sense to set up the training session so that she can succeed. In other words, you want to be sure she can do what you're asking, both physically and emotionally. If not, she'll get frustrated and stop trying and you'll get frustrated and angry and might think your dog is being stubborn, stupid, or just plain lazy. A dog learns quickly when she builds on her successes. But where do you start? At what point do you start training a particular behavior? This brings us to the concept of the "learning baseline."

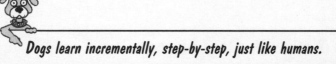

Dogs learn incrementally, step-by-step, just like humans.

When we talk about a dog's learning baseline, we are referring to the dog's starting point. A puppy or an untrained, poorly socialized older dog must be taught to sit beginning with the most rudimentary steps, whereas you might be able to start teaching sit to another dog at a more advanced level and, at the outset, include such factors as duration, distance, and/or distractions. This starting point—or learning baseline—varies for each dog. It depends on the dog's age, training history, personality, health, and so on. Basically, the learning baseline refers to the point and the degree to which your dog will interact with you.

For each behavior you teach, it's important that you start at the point on the learning baseline where your dog can succeed. Take "sit," for example. If you adopt a dog that already has some rudimentary training, her learning baseline—the point you start teaching her "sit"—is quite a bit different from a puppy's "sit" baseline, because the puppy hasn't had the same experiences. If you start the puppy at the same point you would for a more experienced dog, she'll quickly become frustrated.

Not only is it important to start at the point where your dog can succeed, it's also important to continually challenge her. If you keep repeating the same level and don't challenge her, she may lose interest in the training session and get bored. It's up to you to be on the lookout for those moments your dog says, "Got it! This is exciting. What else is there?" That's when you take her to the next level of training for that particular behavior. This awareness distinguishes a really talented trainer—one who is constantly looking to push the envelope and challenge a dog. And just as your dog progresses, your awareness will also reach new levels so you will intuitively know when to "reset" your dog's learning baseline for each individual behavior. Sometimes this happens several times in one session; sometimes it takes several sessions. Now you're becoming a behavioral team. This is when the synergy is born. An example of the learning baseline is found on page 145, in the section on Handling.

How to Work with These Lessons

Let's go through some training exercises just as they are taught in my classes. When you train a dog, start with the simple stuff and go from there. First, you'll learn about handling, in which you gradually help your dog to adapt and to enjoy being touched, then you'll learn how to teach your dog basic behaviors. These lessons are set up in a progressive fashion, which conforms to the way dogs learn; therefore, I suggest you teach the behaviors in the order in which they are presented.

You may find that your daily schedule will allow you to teach three or four of these behaviors in several training sessions throughout the day. If so, start with these three or four and then gradually add more behaviors to your daily regimen. In each subsequent training session, you will make the behaviors you've already taught more and more challenging, while also adding new behaviors.

For most behaviors, you will go through a series of levels, starting with the easiest and progressing to the more advanced. For example, first your dog will learn the beginner's "sit." It is done with a hand signal, using a lure, in one room of your home, and with only you present. That's Level 1. Then, as you progress, you'll go through more challenging levels. In each level you will be adding the three Ds—duration, distance, and distractions—until finally your dog will *reliably* sit wherever and whenever you ask, no matter how long you ask him to sit, how far away you are when you ask him, or how many distractions are present. (See the 3 Ds on page 102.) Of course, it's important to remember that a "reliable" behavior means that your dog will respond to your signal for that behavior at least 80 percent of the time. (See the 80 Percent Rule on page 98.) Level 4, the advanced training for any specific behavior, is further than most people go in training their dogs. It's up to you—you can take your dog to the level of training you choose.

When to go to the next level or add new behaviors: If you are working with your dog several sessions a day, you can add a new behavior whenever you think your dog is ready. That's where the 80 percent rule comes in—when your dog gives you the behavior you request 80 percent of the time over several sessions, you can kick it up a level, going from Level 1 to 2 and so on. Or you can also add new behaviors to your daily sessions following this rule: When your dog performs a Level 1 sit 80 percent of the time you ask him, go on to Level 2 of sit. Then, at the same time, you might want to add Level 1 of the next behavior, which is lie down.

It's not rocket science—you can progress to the next behavior whenever you and your dog feel ready for it. Remember, you will be repeating each of the behaviors learned in previous lessons, only doing more advanced versions of each of these behaviors as you progress through the levels.

Remember: Dogs learn on a curve. They have good days and bad days, just like us. They need time to integrate what they've learned. Each day, begin each exercise at your dog's learning baseline, that is, his starting point. Build on success.

ILLUSTRATION 13

THE ⑤ EASY STEPS TO SHAPE RELIABLE BEHAVIOR

Warm Up

Make sure there is very little distraction in the environment.
Set your goals.
Do a round of the Complete Breath Exercise.
Gather $10,000 rewards.
Rev up your clicker.

1 Start Simple

You can encourage your dog and get her attention by using vocal sounds (such as "teh-teh") or whistling; or motion, such as clapping your hands or patting your leg. Start with simple forms of the behavior you are working on and continuously reinforce (reward) every successful response. Do 10-15 repetitions of each behavior over several sessions. Use a food lure if necessary.

2 Increase distance of reward

When you're 80% sure your dog will do the behavior without using the food lure, put the treat in your other hand. Make the hand signal, click the behavior, and reward from your other hand. Repeat 10 to 15 times for several sessions.

3 Begin using vocal cue

When you're 80% sure your dog will sit each time you make the hand signal, begin to use the word "sit" immediately before using the hand signal. Repeat.

4 Begin varying rewards (and times when you reward)

Begin variable reinforcement schedule. Reward the behavior every 2nd or 3rd time or after 2 or 3 behaviors in a row (sit, sit, *reward*, sit, down, sit, *reward*) Mix it up. Vary the value of the treats; use a $10,000 treat (like turkey) only for the best behavior. Use lesser valued rewards at various other times.

5 Begin adding 3 D's, one at a time

Begin adding duration, distance, and distractions one at a time. Every time you add something new, go back to easy forms of the behavior and reward *every* successful response. Gradually progress to a variable reward schedule, as in Step 4 above, then progress to intermittent reward schedule.

As you'll see in the chart, The 5 Steps to Shape Reliable Behavior, the steps to training any behavior are the same. You start with simple forms of a behavior and, as your dog becomes more successful, you add more challenges. The more your dog repeats the behavior, the more reliable that behavior gets. Simply follow the steps as outlined in this model every time you teach a new behavior.

> *Note:* *If your dog does something other than what you're asking for, you've gone too far, too fast. Return to simpler forms of the behavior, increasing your dog's successful responses, and then ask for more.*

Using a Clicker as a Marker

I prefer to use a clicker as a "marker" for several reasons. (See Markers on page 104.) If you don't have a clicker, use a vocal cue such as "perfect" or "that's it" or a hand signal such as the okay sign or the thumbs-up sign whenever the instructions tell you to click.

Prepare Yourself Before Each Training Session

Before each training session take a minute or two to do the following preparation work—or do the communication exercise on page 85:

1. Tense all the muscles in your body at once. Hold for three seconds and then relax and let your body go limp. Make fists with your hands and make a fist with your face. (Refer to Illustration 3 on page 64.) Then relax.
2. Do one complete round of the complete breath exercise (see page 65).
3. Think about each of the behaviors you are going to work on in the upcoming session. With your eyes closed, spend ten seconds picturing your dog in the final position of each behavior. (For more detailed instructions, review Step 5 of the communication exercise in Chapter 5 on page 86.)

Handling

Handling is an important socialization exercise that helps teach your dog to adapt to her environment. It includes teaching your dog to enjoy being stroked, touched, petted, and held. Although some people wouldn't consider handling to be a behavior, the fact is that when your dog learns to be handled he is learning to do something—hence, it is a behavior. Handling is important not only for vet-friendly visits so your dog will allow an examination, but also to create a safe environment. This is especially important if there are children in your home. If a dog has not learned to be handled or touched and a child should happen to step on the tail or accidentally fall on the dog, the dog might react by biting the child. I can't emphasize this enough. In a recent case in Los Angeles, a fourteen-month-old child wandered into the backyard, petted the family's dog on the head, and was severely bitten. Obviously, this dog had not been properly socialized, let alone trained what to do when a baby enters the yard, such as lie down. Tragically, the baby died. Unfortunately, this is not a rare occurrence.

From puppies to adult dogs, it's up to each handler to ascertain to what degree the dog is comfortable being touched, if at all. It's at this point, which I call the handling baseline, that you begin to work with tactile socialization with your dog. In The Learning Baseline for Handling chart on page 145 (Illustration 14), the handling baseline ranges from Point A, in which a dog allows minimal interaction to Point F, in which a dog is supremely secure in his interactions with you. When other people touch the dog, each person must begin at an earlier handling stage and gradually progress.

A poorly socialized dog *does not like*:

- being touched or petted on the head;
- having a person reach over his body or touch his back;
- having a person reach out to him, especially if he is backing up;
- having his paws or tail touched.

ILLUSTRATION 14

THE LEARNING BASELINE:
FOR HANDLING

The *learning baseline* refers to the point at which the dog is motivated to interact with you. This chart illustrates the learning baseline for handling, ranging from Point A in which the dog has minimal interaction to Point F in which the dog is supremely secure in his interactions with you. You never want to distress your dog by asking her to do more than is physically, mentally, and emotionally possible. Looking at this chart, where would you begin to successfully touch, hold and handle your dog?

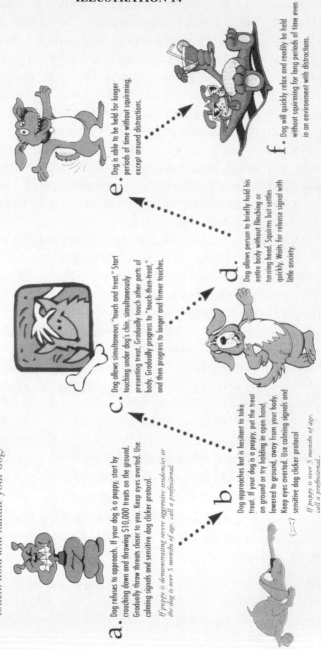

a. Dog refuses to approach. If your dog is a puppy, start by crouching down and throwing $10,000 treats on the ground. Gradually throw threats closer to you. Keep eyes averted. Use calming signals and sensitive dog clicker protocol.

If puppy is demonstrating severe aggressive tendencies or the dog is over 5 months of age, call a professional.

b. Dog approaches but is hesitant to take treat. If your dog is a puppy, put the treat on ground or try holding in open hand, lowered to ground, away from your body. Keep eyes averted. Use calming signals and sensitive dog clicker protocol

If puppy is over 5 months of age, call a professional.

c. Dog allows simultaneous "touch and treat." Start touching under dog's chin, simultaneously presenting treat. Gradually touch other parts of body. Gradually progress to "touch-then-treat," and then progress to longer and firmer touches.

d. Dog allows person to briefly hold his entire body without flinching or turning head. Squirms but settles quickly. Waits for release signal with little anxiety.

e. Dog is able to be held for longer periods of time without squirming, except around distractions.

f. Dog will quickly relax and readily be held without squirming for long periods of time even in an environment with distractions.

Caution: If your dog is sensitive to touch or motion, shy and stand-offish, please exercise caution to avoid being bitten. Please consult your vet and a behavioral specialist.

You can't expect a dog that has been poorly socialized to immediately accept a human's touch, let alone enjoy being held for any length of time. Point A on the chart illustrates such a dog. This is the type of dog that stays well outside the tactile arena. She wants nothing to do with being touched. Yet, she will interact. She will accept food, but on her own terms. In order to socialize such a dog for handling, start by sitting on the ground, keeping your side to the dog, and use body language that communicates a nonthreatening demeanor. This body language includes looking away, scratching, blinking, licking your lips, yawning, and so on. Next, throw a $10,000 treat like a piece of turkey toward the dog, but off to the side. Then throw several more treats, one at a time. During each session, throw the treat a little closer, so the dog will gradually gravitate toward you.

In each stage, using a clicker can speed the training process along. However, since most dogs that show this degree of sensitivity and shyness are equally sensitive to sound, it's important to use the clicker protocol for sensitive dogs because you don't want to make the situation worse. (See notes on using a clicker on page 105.)

At Point B on the chart we have a dog that will take a treat close to you but whose back end seems to be straining to stay away at the same time that the front end leans forward to take the treat. Gradually, treat by treat, inch by inch, entice the dog to reach over your body to take the treat. Never reach for a dog. Always let the dog choose to come to you except, of course, in an emergency.

> *Note:* *Please use a behavioral specialist if your dog is exhibiting truly "standoffish" behavior such as indicated in Points A and B on the Learning Baseline chart for Handling. Always err on the side of safety to avoid being bitten or the possibility that a member of your family, especially a child, might be bitten.*

At Point C touch is added to the equation. However, it's important that you don't rush the process. Ask the dog to lean toward you and take the treat from one hand while you simultaneously touch him with the other hand. Always start touching under the chin because, as I mentioned earlier, some dogs don't like it when people reach over their bodies.

(See Illustration 15.) Gradually, over several sessions, begin touching other parts of the body, going from the head, down the back, to the tail and paws. After every touch, reward your dog.

ILLUSTRATION 15

Handling: Illustrations 15 and 16 show Point C of the Handling Baseline. In 15, handling consists of a simultaneous touch and treat beginning under the dog's chin.

ILLUSTRATION 16

In 16, you progress to touching over the dog's head. This progression will take several sessions with a dog that will interact at this level and is not too stressed.

ILLUSTRATION 17

In Illustration 17, the dog is now at Point D.

ILLUSTRATION 18

Illustration 18 represents a dog that is at Point F.

Once you become successful with the simultaneous touch *and* treat, start to touch and *then* treat, beginning with a one-second delay. Next, begin touching for longer periods of time with longer delays between the touches and the treats. Then progress to firmer touches, gradually touching all over the dog's body. Once again, reward the dog after every touch.

The next stage, Point D, is a dog that allows someone to touch and hold his body without flinching or turning his head. At this point, the dog can be held for several seconds and briefly lifted off the ground. He may squirm initially but he settles down quickly. Be sure to continue giving rewards after every attempt at holding him.

At Point E, the dog has lost his anxiety about being held or lifted and has shifted his focus onto the reward. The occasional squirm or tenseness is triggered again when major distractions come up but, at this point, the dog will quickly settle down again. Now he has begun to look at most touching and holding as enjoyable.

The final stage is when the dog really loves being touched and held and welcomes every friendly fondle. Now the touch has become its own reward.

Start simple. Begin training in a nondistracting environment so you can set your dog up for success. Later, as your dog becomes more and more successful, add distractions one at a time.

Targeting

Note: Your dog must be used to working with a clicker or other marking sound or motion before you start targeting. (See Markers— Clickers, Whistles, and Words on page 104.)

Targeting is the use of any object or sound, including your own hand, that the dog focuses on as a part of the training process. The use of targeting as a learning tool is described in Chapter 6 on page 108, and targets and target sticks are described in Chapter 8 on page 125. Targeting is an important tool because it makes learning so easy for your dog. Your dog will know exactly where to go and, with very little effort, what to do. Targeting is used to teach heeling, sit, down, stand, jump through hoops, go through tunnels, and a host of other behaviors. Here's how to introduce a target stick to your dog:

1. Start in a nondistracting environment. Rub the colored end of the target stick with some turkey and present the stick a few inches away so your dog isn't threatened by this new object. As soon as she explores the stick by sniffing, click, praise, and treat.

2. Because you are already 80 percent sure your dog will put her nose on the stick because of its smell, you can say the word

"touch" immediately before putting the stick in front of her. To sum up: Say "touch" and present the stick three or four inches from your dog's nose. When she touches it, click, treat, and remove the stick. Repeat.

3. After several sessions, begin moving the stick around so she really has to move to touch it.

4. Use the exact same process to teach your dog to touch your hand or your index finger.

ILLUSTRATION 19

Targeting is a terrific tool to help your dog learn what you want her to do. This series of photos illustrate how dogs can be taught to "target" your hand or a stick for heeling.

ILLUSTRATION 20

ILLUSTRATION 21

The target can also be used to teach your dog virtually anything, from jumping over a pole (as shown), to climbing up on things, running through tunnels, finding lost keys, and getting a soda out of the refrigerator.

Note: *If your dog is sensitive to sound or motion, offer the target stick at a level below her head. You can do this by simply sitting on the floor.*

Keep most of your training sessions short—no more than five to ten minutes. Do ten to fifteen repetitions of each behavior.

By the way, you're doing great. You deserve a reward too. Go into the kitchen right now and grab a delicious piece of fruit! (Or warm up a piece of apple pie.)

Pay Attention

A big reason your dog doesn't do what you ask, when you ask, is due to her lack of attention. To motivate a dog you've got to get her attention first. This entire book is geared toward linking up with your dog. When you're linked, both you and your dog are paying attention to each other.

Every day you inadvertently trigger your dog's attention when you open a bag of dog food, open the door to go outside, pick up the leash, put your jacket on, and so on. Without formally training her to do so, you have established a "pay attention" behavior. You have turned a switch on in your dog's head that signals to her that something good is about to happen and she looks to you for that event.

To get your dog to pay attention to you whenever you ask, follow these steps:

1. Place a lure in your hand and hold it in front of your dog's nose. (See Lures, Bribes, and Rewards on page 96.)
2. Move your hand to your eyes in a smooth gesture, while simultaneously saying "watch" or "pay attention" or "look." As your dog's eyes follow your hand going up to your face, click and reward. Repeat these steps.
3. When you are 80 percent sure your dog will follow your hand motion, you are ready for the next step, in which you put the treat in your other hand. (This is to ensure that your dog is following the signal, rather than being bribed by the food. The food should only be a reward, not a bribe.) Place your empty hand in front of your dog's nose and repeat as above, using the same marker word such as "look" as you move your hand to your eyes. Click and treat *from the other hand*. Repeat.
4. When you are 80 percent sure your dog will follow the vocal cue only, begin to "fade" the hand signal. This means gradually shorten the movement you are using from the dog's nose to the eyes, to just pointing to your eyes, and, finally, to using no movement at all.
5. Add the three Ds—duration, distance, and distractions (see page 102). Go back to using a lure if necessary whenever a new element is introduced in the behavior.

Note: *You can drop a treat from your mouth to help your dog learn the vocal cue without the hand signal. Say "look" and as your dog looks at your face, let the treat drop from your mouth. This will help her focus on your face because that's where the $10,000 reward is coming from.*

> *For each behavior, as your dog gets more and more successful, "fade" the rewards. That is, move from a continuous reinforcement schedule to an intermittent reinforcement schedule. (See Reinforcement Schedules on page 103.)*

Sit

Sit—Level 1

1. Begin in an environment that has few distractions or no distractions at all.
2. Put a treat between your thumb and palm. Hold the clicker in your other hand, away from your dog's face. Using the finger target technique, put your hand over the top of your dog's nose about two inches away. Go no farther than the crown of his head. The idea is to get your dog to tilt his head and look up at your hand. As he looks up, his back end will tend to go down. If you move your hand too far, he'll back up. If you move your hand too high, he might jump to get the treat. If you move your hand too low, he won't do anything except nibble your hand. You can encourage him all the while with "gooooood dog," "you're the best," "way to go," or the phrase of your choosing in a friendly but not too exuberant voice. As soon as his behind hits the floor, click and treat and praise! Repeat these steps ten to fifteen times in each training session. *Note: If you're having a problem getting your dog to sit, use approximations by rewarding every behavior that is a small part of sitting, such as looking up, leaning back, or when his rear end almost touches the floor. (All of these are steps in the process of sitting.) After every successful part of the behavior, reward and gradually ask for more the next time.*

3. When you are 80 percent sure your dog will sit whenever you begin to move your hand, begin saying "sit" *just before* you move your hand.
4. Repeat the sessions 3 to 5 times a day and do approximately 15 repetitions of each behavior for up to 2 or 3 minutes. Also incorporate the sit behavior into your dog's daily routine. Have her sit before going indoors and outdoors, up and down the stairs, before being let out of her kennel, and so on. In these examples, the reward is the freedom to be with you. You don't have to use treats.

Note: *If your dog jumps instead of sitting, use the no-reward marker. Say "oops" or "uh-oh" and very quickly pull the treat away. As soon as he is on all fours again, immediately begin the process over, moving your hand over his head and continuing to encourage him. (See "No-Reward" Markers on page 107.)*

Sit—Level 2

Now you will add distance and a low-level distraction so your dog will learn to sit when you're not right by her side.

1. Face your dog. Using the methods in Level 1, have her sit one foot away from you. Repeat several times, then increase the distance to 2 feet, then 3 feet, etc. Continue adding distance until you can get her to sit from 50 feet away.
2. Have your dog sit in front of you. Move your right foot and step to her side; move back, then click and treat. If she's successful in staying put, go one step farther by her side and then move back to the beginning, standing in front of her. Click and treat. Continue until you're able to walk all the way around your dog one step at a time. For some dogs it's easier to do this if they're in a down position. Just go at your dog's own speed. Once you get all the way around, give her a jackpot! Reward with four or five treats one after another, all the while telling her how great she is. Keep the sessions short. Use great treats to start and progress to low-value treats and then just give one every so often.

3. Introduce the automatic "sit": Start in an environment with no distractions, like your backyard. Have her walk by your side. Every time you stop, have her sit, using the vocal cue, the hand cue, or both. Click and reward each success. If she doesn't sit within two seconds, say "oops" or "nope" (the no-reward marker) and walk a few more steps. Try again. A good way to add distractions to the automatic sit is when you take your dog on walks, such as when you get to a curb. Here's another suggestion: Ask a good-natured neighbor for a few minutes of his time and then go outdoors with your dog. You and the neighbor should begin walking toward each other. Then stop and have your dog sit while your neighbor keeps coming toward you. If your dog gets up, the neighbor should immediately turn around and go the other way for a few feet, then stop, turn toward you, and wait. If your dog sits, your neighbor should once again begin approaching. As your neighbor reaches you, he (or you) should click and reward and pet your dog. Then gradually extend the length of time your dog is in the "sit-stay."

Sit—Level 3

Now you're ready to add other distractions so your dog will sit in other places and with other things going on in the environment.

1. Have your dog sit while your back is turned toward her. Then say "sit" again while you're lying down, then when you're in a different room, and other variations. Reward after every success. Obviously, this is a gradual process. Progress at your dog's own speed. (Are *you* having fun? Are *you* happy? Keep a good attitude.)
2. Begin introducing other dogs and people to the environment. If she's distracted, interrupt her with a sound such as "uh-oh," "oops," or "nope" and a motion such as waving your hand in front of her face—if necessary, with food in the hand. Put other people and dogs at a distance where she'll successfully follow your cue to sit. Gradually decrease the distance until she'll respond even with another dog right next to her.
3. After a few sessions of this, add another dog in the environment as a distraction. Choose another dog that is pretty well behaved

and knows this routine. Having two dogs learning at the same time is too much to ask. Go back to the beginning of the magnet game (see page 159) and progress from there.

4. You can also practice straddling your dog. While walking around your dog in her stay position, step over her and then walk over her, straddling her so you take one step on one side and another step on the other side.

Sit—Level 4

In Level 4 you will be adding even more duration, distance, and distractions so your dog will sit wherever and whenever you ask.

1. Add duration while asking your dog to sit. Work up to a ten-minute sit. Leave the room or practice in front of the supermarket. *Always* keep your dog in sight and make sure he is on a leash when you're in public places. (See Stay on page 167.)

2. Add distance while asking your dog to sit. Ask him to sit and lie down and then sit again from 50 feet away.

3. Add more distractions while asking your dog to sit. Start training at a distance your dog is successful. Gradually build up the distractions to include loud and sudden noises, such as banging pots, dropping chairs, whistling, people with floppy coats walking by, and bouncing basketballs. Be creative. Practice at the veterinarian's office, the homes of neighbors and relatives, inside the pet store, and at carnivals. Practice hand signals only and then practice voice signals only. Do the "walk around." At this level, you have progressed to walking around your dog with another dog, you're able to straddle your dog and walk over your dog while banging a drum or wearing a floppy coat, or both. Strangers can also walk over your dog if you've put her in a sit-stay.

> *Use a "no-reward" marker like "oops" or "uh-oh" when your dog doesn't do what you want.*

ILLUSTRATION 22

With a treat in one hand and a clicker in the other, introduce your dog to a sit by bringing your hand with the treat over the top of your dog's nose. Practice using "approximations," if necessary.

ILLUSTRATION 23

If your dog jumps out of her position, use a "no-reward" marker such as "uh-oh" or "oops" to let her know that isn't what you're looking for. Always build on success.

ILLUSTRATION 24

At this point you and your dog have progressed to a Level 2 "automatic sit." Every time you stop, have your dog sit by your side until she does it automatically.

ILLUSTRATION 25

In a Level 3 sit, add more and more distractions one at a time, such as adding other dogs and people to the environment.

Magnet game

Reward-based, nonviolent dog training is all about attraction. It's about creating an environment so your dog can learn how to get your attention by doing behaviors you consider appropriate. On the other side of the coin, she also learns that when she does something other than behaviors that are acceptable to you, she no longer gets your attention. In other words, the "magnetic attraction" is broken. She sits and you praise her; she lies down and you give her a piece of turkey; she goes to her spot and she gets a treat-filled toy or is allowed to go outside. Basically, the magnet game presents your dog with opportunities to receive rewards based on appropriate behaviors.

1. Several times during the day tether your dog to the bottom of the couch or to a door in a social area where you can supervise her. (See Illustrations 10, 11, and 12 on pages 133 and 134 for the proper way to tether your dog to a door.) *Never tether a dog and leave her alone.* She should be allowed about 3 feet of leash but not be able to reach you.

2. Now here's where the magnet part fits in. Whenever she does a particular behavior you want to reinforce, such as sitting or lying down, she becomes a magnet, drawing your attention. At this point you can: (1) throw her a treat; (2) praise her; (3) get up and pet her; or (4) combine all three as a triple-reward. If she gets up from the sit or down position, immediately withdraw your attention. (At this point, she is no longer a magnet attracting your attention.) So let's say she sits, which is the behavior you are looking for and you start to get up to go over and pet her. However, as you're on the way to pet her, she gets up. Since sitting is the behavior you want, not standing, the magnetic attraction has been broken because she got up. At this point, you should immediately turn around and go the other way. If she sits or lies down again, you should immediately begin walking toward her again because the magnet is working again.

This is a great exercise to do while you're watching television, talking on the phone, eating dinner, or working at your desk. We use it in group classes all the time. As long as a dog is sitting or lying down, the handler stays by her side. But if she gets up, the handler moves away. Dogs pick this up very quickly and it really helps in the overall training process.

You will understand better how the magnet game works if you do a human version of it with a friend. Let's say the two of you are just sitting around talking. Both of you should think of one behavior you want to reinforce in the other person but *keep it secret* from the other person. In other words, you're both playing the game and you're both "it." For example, you might choose to reinforce a smile, a scratch on the head, a look out the window, a yawn, tapping the toe, or biting a fingernail. Now each one of you decide on a "marker," that is, the sound that you are going to use to "mark" the other person's behavior whenever he happens to do the behavior you are looking for. (See Markers on page 104.) It might be "ahhh," "way to go," "nice job," or any number of words or phrases you decide upon. Now, as the visit progresses, every time one of you sees the other do the desired behavior, quickly say the word or phrase. In most cases, just like your dog, the person won't remember what he just did that elicited your response. However, after a number of repetitions, he will connect your marker with his behavior. The first one to figure out the behavior gets a reward. Be creative! This is actually a pretty fun game and it can certainly help you understand the way your dog learns.

ILLUSTRATION 26

Magnet Game: The Magnet Game consists of waiting for your dog to figure out what you want without your having to ask for it. In these photos, Orbit, a Chinese Crested, is being ignored because she is standing up on her bed.

ILLUSTRATION 27

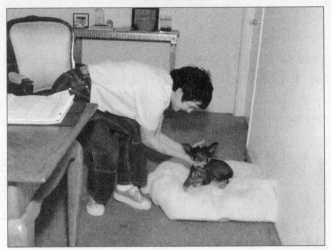

As soon as she lies down without being told, she is immediately rewarded with praise, treats, and affection.

Lie Down

Lie down—Level 1

1. Begin in a nondistracting environment. Start with your dog in a sit position. Present your hand with a treat just under her nose and move it straight to the ground. Imagine there's an invisible string attached to your hand and your dog's nose, as though you're pulling her nose to the ground. Verbally encourage her. At the moment she lies down, click, praise, and treat. Repeat ten to fifteen times.

2. When you are 80 percent sure your dog will lie down whenever you present the hand signal, begin to say the word "down" *immediately* before doing the hand signal. If your dog just isn't "getting it," use "approximations," or simpler forms of the down behavior. For instance, if you're training a puppy, you can click and treat the first "approximation" represented by her head lowering a few inches. Then you can click and treat her when she lowers her head lower *and* moves a paw forward. Then you can click and treat the final behavior when she goes all the way down. If your dog gets up from the sit, quickly withdraw the treat, say "oops" and start again. But go a little slower because you want to build on success.

TIP

If you're having an especially difficult time getting your dog to lie down, here are a couple of tips to encourage her. Lead your dog to the top of the stairs. Hold a treat in front of her and lower it down toward the first step so she has to reach to get it. Or, as an alternative, sit on the floor with your legs stretched out in front of you. Then bend one of your legs so the knee is up in the air and the foot is on the floor. Now you have created the entrance of a tunnel. Using a treat, lure your dog into the tunnel so she'll have to lower her body to reach the treat as she reaches under your leg. In this way, she is encouraged to do the beginning stages of "lie down."

Lie Down—Level 2

Now you're ready to add distance and duration to the lie down behavior.

1. Practice having your dog lie down from his standing position.
2. Practice having your dog lie down from a distance. Begin by standing 1 foot away, then 2 feet, and so on.
3. Extend the length of time your dog is in a down position to five minutes. Once again, build on success. Start with a few seconds and build to five minutes. Take your time. Smile.
4. Teach her to sit from a down position. Imagine that an invisible string is attached from her nose to your hand. Begin with a treat in your hand and slowly move it straight up. Click and reward. Then practice "sit-ups": *sit, down, sit, down.* Click, praise, and reward. Repeat these steps.

Lie Down—Level 3

Now you're ready to add distractions so your dog will lie down in other places and with other things going on in the environment.

1. Have your dog lie down while your back is turned toward him. Then say "lie down" again while you're lying down, when you're in another room, and other variations. Obviously, this is a gradual process. Progress at your dog's speed.

2. Begin introducing other dogs and people to the environment. If he's distracted, interrupt him with a sound such as "uh-oh," "ooops," or "nope" and a motion such as waving your hand in front of his face—if necessary, with food in the hand. Put other people and dogs at a distance where he'll successfully follow your cue. Gradually decrease the distance until he'll respond even with another dog right next to him.

3. Arrange a time to meet a neighbor outdoors. Begin walking toward each other. Stop and have your dog lie down while your neighbor keeps coming toward you. If your dog gets up, the neighbor should immediately turn around and go the other way for a few feet, then stop, turn toward you, and wait. If your dog lies down, your neighbor should once again begin approaching. As your neighbor reaches you, he (or you) should click and reward and pet your dog. Then gradually extend the "lie down–stay."

4. After a few sessions doing this, instead of stopping and waiting for the neighbor to approach, continue until you meet. Click and reward when your dog lies down.

Teach an Automatic "Lie Down" for Child Safety

Integrate the automatic "lie down" if you have a baby or small child in the house. Start in an environment with no distractions. Tether your dog or have another person hold the leash. Walk into the room carrying your baby or child, or, if she's old enough to walk, have her walk by your side. Every time you walk in the room with the child, ask your dog to lie down using the vocal cue, the hand cue, or both. Click and reward each success. Repeat these steps. If the baby is old enough, progress to the point of allowing her to go in the room by herself. When the child enters, your dog should either lie down and stay until released or go into another room or her kennel. Safety for your dog is as important as safety for your child.

Lie Down—Level 4

In Level 4 you will be adding even more distance and distractions so your dog will lie down wherever and whenever you ask.

1. Add duration while asking your dog to lie down. Work up to a thirty-minute lie down. Leave the room or practice in front of the supermarket. *Always* keep your dog in sight and on a leash when you're in public places.

2. Add more distractions while asking your dog to lie down. Start training at a distance where your dog is successful. Gradually build up the distractions to include loud and sudden noises, such as banging pots, dropping chairs, whistling, people wearing floppy coats, multiple dogs, and bouncing basketballs. Practice at the veterinarian's office, the homes of neighbors and relatives, inside the pet store, and at carnivals. Practice hand signals only and then practice voice signals only. Do the "walk around"—at this level, you should be able to walk around your dog with another dog in tow.

3. Add distance while asking your dog to lie down. Ask her to sit and lie down and then sit again from 50 feet away.

Vary the rewards and vary the value of the rewards.

ILLUSTRATION 28

In teaching your dog to lie down, use hand signals first, with lots of praise and $10,000 rewards.

ILLUSTRATION 29

When you are 80 percent certain she will lie down whenever you signal, begin adding the word "down" immediately before the hand signal.

ILLUSTRATION 30

Stand

Teaching your dog to stand is really helpful for visits to the veterinarian, when wiping your dog's paws, and for grooming and washing. It only takes a second.

Stand—Level 1

1. Place your dog in a sit, facing you.
2. Put a lure in your hand and place your hand directly in front of your dog's nose, palm forward.
3. Say "stand" and slowly draw your hand away from his nose, moving your hand parallel to the ground. Why are you saying "stand" at this point? Remember, you want to label the behavior with the word for it when you are 80 percent sure your dog will do it. In this case, the dog is following your hand with a treat in it and you are in a nondistracting environment, so you are already 80 percent sure he will do it.
4. As your dog gets up to take the treat, click, praise, and reward.
5. Repeat.

Stand—Level 2

Gradually add duration by asking your dog to stand for longer periods of time.

Stand—Level 3

Add distance by moving farther away from your dog when you ask him to stand.

Stand—Level 4

Add distractions by asking your dog to stand in various environments. Walk around and over her. Touch her all over her body.

Focus on what you want; don't focus on what you don't want.

Stay

Some trainers don't teach the "stay" behavior. They feel once you've told your dog to sit or lie down, he should remain in that position until released. The theory is perfectly sound, but I find most people forget to release their dogs and the dogs end up releasing themselves. So I include the word "stay" in all of the exercises—not only for the dog's benefit but mostly for the human's.

Remember, every exercise or behavior has a start and a finish. You must first signal the behavior and then release your dog from the behavior. We do this in a fun way, of course. I use the word "okay" as a release word, although some trainers feel the word "okay" is used so often in our daily vocabulary that the dog might hear the word somewhere in the environment and take off. So if you prefer, pick another release word, like "free." But "okay" is okay for me, okay?

1. Signal your dog to do any behavior (sit, lie down, stand, etc.).
2. Say "stay." (Why are you saying "stay" at this point? Remember, for some exercises you don't want to label a behavior with the word—in this case, "stay"—until you are 80 percent sure your dog will perform the behavior when requested. But at this point in the training you are only asking the dog to "stay" for a half-second, so you're already 80 percent sure he'll do it.)
3. With your clicker in one hand, put the palm of your other hand in front of your dog's nose and click, praise, and treat. The click, with the word "okay" or "free," releases your dog. Gradually proceed to asking him to stay for one full second, then two seconds, and so on. Eventually you'll stop using the clicker and just use the word "okay" or "free," to signify the end of the exercise and release your dog.

Levels 2, 3, and 4 of stay simply include longer duration, greater distance, and more distractions as noted in the exercises themselves.

Use management, not punishment. (See Managing Your Dog, page 133.)

Hide-and-Seek Game

This game is similar to the hide-and-seek we all played as children.

Hide-and-Seek—Level 1

1. Simply ask your dog to sit or lie down and stay.
2. Now run behind a chair and hide for one second.
3. Stick your head out and say "peek-a-boo!"
4. When your dog runs to you, really praise her and make a big deal out of how clever she was in finding you.

Hide-and-Seek—Level 2

Gradually make the basic game more challenging by asking for longer "stays" and making yourself more difficult to find. For example, run into your bedroom and hide in the closet. To make it easy at first, keep the door open a few inches. Get other people involved and have them say "Find Jane! Where's Jane?"

Hide-and-Seek—Level 3

Now jump up—gingerly, of course—on a chest of drawers. Challenge your dog to find you "up in the air." Add distractions.

Hide-and-Seek—Level 4

When you're out on a walk, put your dog on a 40-foot leash. When she isn't looking, quickly hide behind a tree or climb up a tree. She will not only love the game, but you'll also be teaching her to keep you in sight. Work in a distracting environment such as a park with dogs and other animals. Use caution! Always have a friend hold your dog while you go to hide and never leave your dog unattended.

Find It

This is a great training exercise because it stimulates your dog's emotional, mental, and physical nature.

Find It—Level 1

1. Ask your dog to sit.

2. Immediately put a $10,000 treat—like a piece of turkey—on the floor in front of him and say "find it."
3. Repeat this several times, progressively moving the treat farther away, but still in plain view. (If your dog starts to get up in anticipation, you'll have to work on getting him to stay until you release him with the words "find it.")

Find It—Level 2

1. Progressively add more distance, until you are 3 feet from your dog.
2. Next, "hide" the treat behind the leg of a table or chair or behind a footstool. In other words, let him see you place it, but put it somewhere just out of sight. Then say "find it" and he'll look at you as if you're kidding. He'll promptly go to the treat. When he gobbles it up, praise him to high heaven for being such a brilliant dog.

Find It—Level 3

1. In each subsequent session, place the treats in harder to find locations.
2. Then progress to having your dog stay in one room while you go into another room and hide the treat. Gradually make it more and more challenging by hiding treats under a throw rug or on a windowsill where your dog can just reach it.

Find It—Level 4

1. Move the whole routine outdoors. Begin with easy finds and progress to making it more and more challenging. Try this variation: Before you take your dog outside, shuffle your feet on the lawn to make a "track." Drop a treat somewhere along the track. Then bring your dog to the beginning of the track and tell him to "find it." Your dog will learn to pick up your scent from the track marks your shoes made and follow your scent to the treat.
2. Use "find it" to keep your dog occupied finding treats while you take your morning shower or have a leisurely breakfast. Hide as many as twenty treats around the house or out in the yard. Or, hide lots of treats around the house just before you leave for work and then say "find it" as you go out the door.

He'll soon learn to eagerly await your departure every day. (Obviously, this second suggestion will only work if your dog is trustworthy and it's safe to allow him freedom to roam the house without destroying it.)

> *Note:* Remember to adjust your dog's regular diet to account for daily treats!

Go to Your Spot

This behavior is used to teach your dog to go any particular place you want. The methods are exactly the same to teach him to go to his kennel, bed, blanket, mat, den, etc. Simply change the word accordingly.

Go to your spot is one of the handiest and most useful behaviors you can ask your dog to do. It can help in many different types of situations, such as when your dog barks at the mail carrier, nudges you while you're on the phone, races to the door when the doorbell rings, begs at the dinner table, or acts fearful about strangers working around the house. By directing your dog to "go to your spot," you are redirecting his attention and giving him something else to do. This can help calm him if he's nervous or distract him when he's doing something you don't want him to do. There's also a very practical use of this behavior when your dog is in your way. For instance, you can avoid tripping over him when you have a heavy laundry basket in your hands by asking him to go to a specific place.

Going step-by-step, your dog will pick up this behavior very quickly.

1. Stand no more than 1 foot away from the place you want your dog to use as a "spot" (or bed, blanket, den, or other place you want to teach him to go to).
2. Say the word you want your dog to associate with that place, such as "spot" or "go to your place." (I use the phrase "park it.") With a $10,000 treat in your hand, let your dog see you throw the treat onto the spot. Or, instead of using a treat as a lure, you can point to the spot with your target stick (see Illustrations 33

and 34 on page 174). (Why are you labeling the behavior with the word "spot" at this point? Remember, for most exercises you don't want to label a behavior with the word—in this case, "spot"—until you are 80 percent sure your dog will perform the behavior when requested. But, with this particular behavior, you are already almost 100 percent sure your dog is going to successfully respond by following the treat to the spot.)

3. As soon as your dog gets to the spot to get the treat, click and give praise. *Note: For shy or hesitant dogs, click the smallest approximation of the behavior. In this case, click when one paw goes on the spot; click again with another attempt when two paws go on the spot, and so on.*

4. Repeat several times over several sessions.

5. Depending on your dog's progress, when you reach a point where you are 80 percent sure your dog will go to her spot when you say "spot" while making the hand motion without throwing the treat, put the treat in your other hand. Give the verbal request and point. Click when your dog is on the spot. Now reward with the treat from your other hand *after* your dog has gone to the spot. The difference here is that you're no longer using the treat as a lure or target. It is now used only as a reward.

6. Begin moving away from the spot, a foot at a time. Once again, every time you increase your distance, you do so because you are 80 percent sure your dog will be successful. If your dog doesn't know what you're asking, it's a good bet you've gone too far too fast. Go back to the point you both were successful and work at that distance a little while longer before increasing the distance.

7. Once you've reached a point where your dog will go to her spot from virtually anywhere, plug in the intermittent reinforcement schedule. Give her a treat every other time, then every third or fourth time, etc. Start varying the value of the rewards; in addition to food rewards, include rewards such as going for a walk or a ride. When you add a distraction, like meeting someone at the door, go back to standing right by the spot, use $10,000 treats again and go back to rewarding every time. As your dog is more successful, gradually add distance and incorporate the intermittent reward schedule. Once she has really got it, her

reward can be simply getting to meet the person at the door or some other positive reward like getting to go outside with you.

If you really want to get fancy, you can send your dog to four different areas. Be sure to give each area its own individual "label" such as "bed," "mat," "kennel," "couch," etc. Work on the areas one at a time so each behavior is in place before you teach him to go to another area. When you think he knows two different spots, such as the bed and the kennel, start putting them at opposite ends of the same room. Send him to the bed ten times. (You can point to help him out.) Do this for a few sessions, then send him to the kennel. Now, with voice only, say the word without pointing. See what happens. When your dog seems to get it at least 80 percent of the time, start moving the bed and the kennel closer together. Gradually build on success until they are next to each other. Once your dog has this two-item behavior figured out, add the third item such as the mat. Repeat the whole process, starting with the mat on the opposite side of the room.

Teaching a Sensitive Dog to "Go to Your Kennel"

For dogs who are sensitive and really hesitant, there are a number of things you can try:

- If the kennel is the type that is enclosed, take the top off.

- Click systematically. That is, click when your dog puts her head in. Then progress to clicking when one paw goes in, then click again when two paws are in, again when three paws are in, and yet again when all four paws are in.

- Keep the sessions short and make sure the treat is really great. You can also try feeding her meals in the kennel. Leave the food just inside the door to begin with and at each feeding put it farther in until, after a week, she has to go all the way inside to eat. For more sensitive dogs, it's important not to close the kennel gate during this process.

- When she's not looking, put a great treat in the kennel and let her find it on her own throughout the day.

- Don't close the gate until you know she's comfortable being in the kennel. Then, once you close it, only reward her when it is closed. Start with keeping it closed for one second and gradually progress for longer periods of time. Then progress by leaving the room for short periods and gradually increase to longer periods.

ILLUSTRATION 31

Go to Your Spot: Illustrations 31 and 32 show teaching your dog to go to his spot with a hand motion.

ILLUSTRATION 32

ILLUSTRATION 33

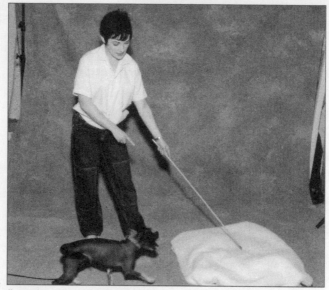

Illustrations 33 and 34 show teaching your dog to go to his spot using a target stick.

ILLUSTRATION 34

Get Off the Couch

To teach your dog to get off the couch or your bed or any other object, use the exact same process as go to your spot. First, let him get on the couch. That shouldn't be too much trouble to arrange. You can do this by verbally encouraging him by saying "couch" or "up" and patting the couch. Don't use a treat to get him on the couch. Once he's on the couch, stand next to it and go through the same steps listed for go to your spot, but instead of saying "couch," say "off."

1. Encourage your dog to get up on the couch or bed.
2. Standing right next to the couch or bed, get your dog's attention by showing her a treat and say "off" while you throw the treat on the floor. Click as soon as all four paws hit the floor. Repeat. (In this case you can label the behavior with the word "off" right away because you are already 80 percent sure she'll do it.)
3. When you are 80 percent sure your dog will get off the couch or bed when you say "off," say "off," click when all four paws hit the floor, and *then* reward. In other words, you are no longer using the treat as a lure. Repeat.
4. When you are 80 percent sure your dog will do this behavior, go to a variable reinforcement schedule by asking for two or three behaviors in a row before rewarding. Then start adding the three D's—duration, distance, and distractions. Then gradually progress to an intermittent reinforcement schedule by rewarding every once in a while.

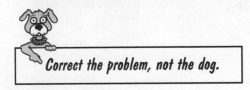

Correct the problem, not the dog.

Come When Called

Remember, the rule is: Never call your dog to you unless you are 80 percent sure she'll respond; don't say "come" if there's a chance she won't. Also, don't call your dog to you if you're going to yell at her or if you're leaving for the day. (In nonviolent training we don't yell anyway, so you should be okay.) If you do this, your dog will very quickly learn that there is a negative consequence whenever she hears the word "come"; hence, she won't come when called. Unless she's at a strong Level 3, never call her if she's running away. She might learn that the word "come" is irrelevant or that "come" means run the other way. (See The 80 Percent Rule on page 98.)

ILLUSTRATION 35

Never call your dog to you unless you are 80 percent sure she'll come when called. Illustration 35 demonstrates Come When Called at Level 1.

ILLUSTRATION 36

Illustration 36 shows Level 2, in which the dog not only comes when called but is asked to sit before being rewarded.

Come When Called—Level 1

1. Crouch down and open your arms.
2. With a happy, excited voice say, "Jackson, come."
3. Click and reward with a treat, affection, praise, and petting when Jackson gets to you.
4. Use everyday opportunities to practice, such as feeding time, going outside, letting him out of the kennel, while you're cooking dinner, etc. While on a walk, periodically repeat this exercise.

Come When Called—Level 2

1. Ask your dog to sit and stay. From a standing position 10 feet away, say with a happy, excited voice, "Jackson, come." As he arrives, click, reward with a treat, affection, praise, and petting and say, "What a wonderful dog you are!"
2. Repeat Step 1, but this time ask your dog to sit in front of you when he arrives, then click and so on. Tell him a joke!
3. Now ask someone else to participate. This step will help teach your dog that rewards come from other places besides you. But your dog still has to listen to you in order to get the reward. Have the participant show your dog the treat. Stand about 3 feet away and begin distracting and enticing your dog with sounds and motions to come to you. Shuffle your feet, crouch down, pat the ground, and open your arms. When your dog moves one or two steps toward you, click, say "okay" and then have the other participant give the reward. Gradually increase your distance from the other person until your dog has to come all the way across the room to you before being given the "okay" to go back to the participant for the reward.
4. This step is an alternative to number 3 above—but without using another participant: Place a treat on the ground 6 feet away. Imagine you're the pitcher, your dog is the batter who is 6 feet away, and the treat is on first base. Happily call your dog. If he comes to you, click, say "okay," and let him get the treat. If he breaks for the treat, say "uh-oh" or "nope" or "oops" or "oh-oh" and quickly run to intercept him. It's important you set it up so you can always get to the treat first. If he does make a break to

"steal first," simply return him to home. Have fun with this. As you take him back to home plate, talk to him with an impish grin. Dogs love humans with impish grins. Say something like this: "I'm watching you like a hawk. Who do you think you are, the dog's bow wow? Hah, have I got your number, Rin Tin Tin!" Hmmm. I'm getting carried away. Let's move on.

5. Practice saying "come" while you're in another room. Practice with your back turned. Practice while you're lying on the ground, while you're sitting on the ground, while standing on your head.

6. Remember, whenever you change environments, you have to go back to the beginning. (See Context Learning in Chapter 6 on page 91.) So when you take your dog outdoors, go back and repeat Level 1. Start in a relatively low distraction environment like the backyard early in the morning.

Come When Called—Level 3

Now you really start adding distractions. *Work indoors first.* Here are two more exercises to integrate:

1. Tell your dog to sit and stay. Use the same great treat that was on first base and move it closer and closer. Your goal is to put it right in the path she has to travel to get to you. She actually has to cross over the treat and sit in front of you and then go back to get the treat when you say "okay." As long as you move the treat incrementally closer, it's easy. Just make sure she's successful at one distance before moving it. Then progress to having another dog in the room. This makes it tough because dogs have a tendency to guard their food. Make sure the other dog is tethered at first.

2. Interrupt her dinner and ask her to come to you. She has to stop eating, sit in front of you, and then go back to eating. Teach this by putting just a little food in the bowl to start. Kibble is best for this exercise. Then call her and reward her with a $10,000 treat like a piece of turkey or liver. Then gradually add more food and add special treats like turkey and liver to the food bowl. If you do this in steps, you no longer will have to reward her from your hand. The food in the bowl will be the reward, even though she stopped eating it to come to you.

3. Now work outdoors again, but move from training in your backyard and early in the morning to a place that is more well trafficked and a time when more people will be around. Start in an environment that isn't too overwhelming. Estimate a distance from other people and dogs where your dog will still respond to you. Gradually decrease the distance by having other dogs get closer and closer. Your goal is to have other dogs walk by within 3 feet. You can then begin to let the other dogs be the reward. Say "okay" and let them play. (Remember to keep your dog on a leash at all times in public places.)

Come When Called—Level 4

Gradually work toward the point where you say "come" while your dog is in the midst of other dogs running and playing. If you follow the step-by-step play sessions, this will all fall in place. Normally a dog is successful doing this between the ages of one and two years, depending on your skill, consistency, and regular practice.

To further strengthen this, play the "retrieve" come when called game. Put your dog by your side. Slowly roll a ball out in front of you. As the ball starts rolling and before she has a chance to chase the ball, immediately call your dog. Click, reward with a treat, and then let her retrieve the ball. Repeat this over and over.

Now throw the ball out and say "okay" as she takes a step toward the ball; say "come" and reward her. Then let her take two steps, three steps, and so on.

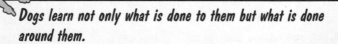

Dogs learn not only what is done to them but what is done around them.

Quiet

Teaching your dog to be quiet can be confusing. This is because the opposite of quiet, barking, is a behavior that really lends itself to being unintentionally trained. (See Unintentional Training on page 201.) In other words, it's easy to inadvertently teach your dog to bark, which is the opposite of the behavior you're looking for. It's therefore important to really watch what you're doing when you interact with your dog in day-to-day situations. For example, if you're on the phone and your dog is barking to get your attention and you finally get fed up and yell "shut up," you may have unintentionally trained him to bark because you gave him the attention he was looking for. Remember, dogs learn "what-happens-when." It's as if they say to themselves, "What happens when I bark?" If the answer is, "I get rewarded by my person paying attention to me," you've just *taught* your dog to bark. So watch how you respond when your dog barks. Try one of the following methods to teach your dog to keep mum.

Believe it or not, an option in teaching your dog to be quiet is to teach him *to bark* when you request it.

1. While your dog is barking use a word like "sing" or "speak." Click, praise, and reward. Do this often enough and pretty soon your dog will have linked barking with the word or signal. (Please note: In this case, you are labeling the behavior right away. This is because your dog is already doing the behavior. The rule is: label something when you are 80 percent sure your dog will do the behavior you are asking for. In this case, your dog is *already* doing the behavior, so go ahead and attach the label "sing" or "speak" to it. Also see Teach Your Dog to Sit Before Labeling It "Sit" on page 100.)
2. Now that your dog is barking on signal, interrupt the barking with another sound, like the word "quiet" or "enough." As soon as she stops barking, click, praise, and reward. Then get her singing again. Then say "quiet" again and click, praise, and treat. Repeat over many days.
3. Keep rewarding the "quiet" behavior with $10,000 treats, but start phasing out the rewards for barking. In this way, you can stretch the length of "quiet" time by rewarding it with really great treats like pieces of turkey. Because you're only using praise to reward the barking, your dog will gravitate toward silence, where the $10,000 is. Now you can shape the behavior by teaching your dog to bark three times and then stop on his own.

Here's another trick you can use. In the preceding exercise you are immediately rewarding the quiet behavior every time you say "quiet." This follows the one-second rule in that you're rewarding the behavior within one second after the dog does it. What happens if your dog stops barking on his own, *without* your signal? If you immediately click and treat, he may view the reward as a reward for barking because you rewarded him within one second of his barking. For that reason, it's important to separate the click and treat by a couple of seconds so he won't make this incorrect association. So count to yourself "one thousand one, one thousand two," *then* click, praise, and treat. Because you've waited at least two seconds after the barking stopped, you're now rewarding what your dog is presently doing—being quiet.

Here's the rule: If you say "quiet," and she responds, click and treat immediately. If she stops barking on her own, wait two seconds, then click and treat.

In group classes we offer the following suggestions for people when their dogs are on a barking jag:

1. Ignore the barking for up to 90 seconds. Many times a dog will bark in excitement when a second dog walks into the class. After a minute or two, the adrenaline rush will subside and the dog will stop barking of his own accord. (This is tool number 1 of the 8 Tools of Dog Training on page 112.)
2. Increase the distance between your dog and the stimulus or block her view from the triggering stimulus. For instance, if your dog is barking at another dog, move her farther away from the other dog. (This is tool number 4 of the 8 Tools of Dog Training on page 114.)
3. Take a walk. If you lead your dog around a chair, you will be taking her mind off the reason for the barking and the barking will stop. (This is both tool number 2 and tool number 5 of the 8 Tools of Dog Training on pages 113 and 115, respectively.)
4. Ask your dog to lie down. A dog often stops barking when placed in a more subordinate position. (This is tool number 2 and tool number 5 of the 8 Tools of Dog Training on pages 113 and 115, respectively.)

5. Interrupt the barking with sound and motion, then praise the quiet behavior. (This is both tool number 5 and tool number 2 of the 8 Tools of Dog Training on pages 115 and 113, respectively.)
6. If your dog is comfortable being handled in distracting environments, hold her to your chest. *Caution: Do not hold a dog in this manner unless she is at least at Point E on the Learning Baseline for Handling (see page 145). See Illustration 37 below.* Repeat as often as necessary. Release your dog only when she has settled down and is quiet. (This is tool number 2 and tool number 5 of the 8 Tools of Dog Training on pages 113 and 115, respectively.)

ILLUSTRATION 37

Illustration 37 shows how to hold a dog to your chest to quiet him. One arm is firmly, but not roughly, wrapped around the back of the dog while the other hand is placed on his head. Note that the thumb is on one side of the dog's ear while the fingers are on the other side. CAUTION: USE THIS METHOD ONLY IF YOUR DOG IS AT POINT E ON THE LEARNING BASELINE FOR HANDLING (SEE PAGE 145).

7. Give her something to chew on to take her mind off the barking. (This is tool number 5 of the 8 Tools of Dog Training on page 115.)
8. Put some peanut butter on the roof of her mouth. (This is tool number 5 of the 8 Tools of Dog Training on page 115.)
9. Teach her to "take it." (See page 193.) Most dogs can't bark with something in their mouths. (This is tool number 2, tool number 5, and tool number 8 of the 8 Tools of Dog Training on pages 113, 115, and 117, respectively.)

Heeling

To many people, the term "heeling" means walking without pulling. However, they are really two separate behaviors. Let's look at the differences:

Heeling means the dog walks or stands by your side within an imaginary boxed area by your leg—not too far ahead of you, not too far behind you, not too far from your side, and not too close to you. The idea is that he stays within the perimeters of this imaginary box, without bumping your leg.

Walking without pulling means just what it says. While the dog is on lead, he can go ahead of you, behind you, or to your side but he immediately stops pulling whenever he feels the slightest tension on the leash.

Remember, don't "label" a behavior until you've already established that behavior. In other words, don't say "heel" until you are 80 percent sure your dog will heel when asked. Also, remember, there are no commands in this training. The words, sounds, and body language you use in training are simply signals. They signal what you want.

There are several methods you can use to teach your dog to walk by your side. You can pick and choose from them or use them in combination.

Heeling—Level 1

1. First, teach your dog to touch a target stick or your index finger. (If necessary, review Targeting on page 108.)

2. Once your dog is touching the stick or your index finger, teach her to heel by simply beginning to walk in a straight line with your finger or the stick in position by your side.
3. When your dog touches the stick or your finger, click and reward. Pretty easy.
4. Then start adding turns and distractions.

If you've worked with targeting, you can say "heel" almost immediately. As you present your finger, say "touch, heel" over and over. Then simply fade the word "touch" and just say "heel."

When you do this in a fenced backyard or other enclosed area, you don't need a leash. This is called "free heeling" because the dog is free to go elsewhere.

Heeling—Level 2

Spontaneous heeling:

1. Meander around an enclosed area or yard with your dog off the leash. If you don't have an enclosed area in which to work, put him on a 20-foot leash so he can wander off.
2. Whenever your dog happens to walk by your side, click, praise, and treat. You can encourage (prompt) him to do this more and more often by patting your leg, taking quick little steps, and praising even the slightest interest. Every time he starts going off in another direction, you should abruptly turn and go the other way, being careful, of course, not to jerk him if he's on lead. Once he gets it, click and treat.

When working with a dog on a leash, I prefer William Campbell's Sof-Touch leash. (See Leashes on page 124.) That way, if your dog does happen to bolt, the shock is severely lessened. Of course, the best bet is not to let that happen.

You can also combine this exercise with the "take it" signal. First, teach your dog to look for a treat by saying "take it" and throwing the treat on the ground. Very quickly he'll learn to start looking for a treat every time you say "take it." Now start meandering around the yard.

Every time he comes near you, say "take it" and throw a treat right by your side. Soon he'll be spending time around your body. This method is especially good for a dog that forges ahead. He'll start holding back as he anticipates the treat.

Note: *If your dog is pulling and he is one of those extra powerful dogs or if he was abused before you got him—as is the case with many rescue dogs—it may be helpful to use a halter-style collar in combination with these methods. I recommend the Premier halter-style collar. (See Appendix C for ordering information.)*

Heeling—Level 3

1. Ask friends, family members, or neighbors to mill around and ask your dog to heel at your side while walking among them.
2. Put environmental distractors around like chairs, garbage cans, safety cones, etc. Ask your dog to heel by your side as you navigate around all of these obstacles doing left turns, right turns, and about turns. Then walk fast and suddenly slow. Stop and start again.

Heeling—Level 4

1. Take your dog to town and ask him to heel as you walk up and down the sidewalk among pedestrians, other dogs, and noisy traffic. Walk over grates, under ladders, and by delivery people who are wheeling carts into stores or restaurants. Remember to keep these sessions short and use $10,000 rewards.
2. Ask for longer periods of heeling.

At this level your dog is riveted to you no matter what and will not leave your side unless released. Most dogs must be somewhere between eighteen and twenty-four months of age to reach this level of proficiency; that is, if you have been working with your dog consistently for a period of at least six months.

Walking Without Pulling

The only difference between "walking without pulling" and "heeling" is that you're allowing your dog a greater freedom area or "envelope." In heeling, you click when the dog is right by your side. In walking without pulling, click and treat whenever your dog is in the general vicinity.

Walking Without Pulling—Level 1

To teach your dog to walk without pulling, first try the start-stop method. Did you ever see a dog straining on a leash, pulling the human along? What's happening here is that the person has inadvertently taught his dog that the freedom to go forward is actually a reward for pulling. This is the exact opposite of what you want your dog to do.

1. The next time your dog pulls, creating a taut leash, stop in your tracks. Your dog will sniff for a while and eventually he'll wonder what's going on.
2. When he turns his head to look back at you, click and immediately begin walking again. Now your dog is learning that a taut leash means stop and a loose leash means go. Each session should be done at a predetermined distance. Use the length of your house to start.
3. After a few trials, say "okay" and let him go to the length of a 20- or 30-foot leash. Every day or two extend the distance you practice by the length of an additional house, until you can walk around the block without a problem. If you try to practice this for too long a period of time, you'll never get around the block. The 20- to 30-foot freedom becomes the reward.

Walking Without Pulling—Level 2

Now, imagine what would happen if your dog voluntarily came back to you.

1. Whenever your dog meanders to your side, click and treat with a $10,000 payoff like a piece of turkey. Freedom is great—maybe it's even worth $5,000 to your dog—but walking by your side

will soon become an even greater motivator. Hence, after a few months, he'll be spending more and more time by your side.

2. As soon as you feel a strong pull, use the start-stop game by simply turning around and walking the other way. If you have a more challenging dog, start out with this game, then add another twist. Your dog, with his desire to walk ahead of you, will quickly make up ground and shoot by you. *Do not jerk!*

3. Now, before he hits the end of the leash again, say "come." The "come" signal will let him know he can control his forward progress, but he has to come to you first. As long as the leash is slack, he can continue. Another thing you can do here is reverse direction. As soon as he passes you, immediately turn and go the other way. Every time he goes to your side, click, praise, and reward. This click marks the position you're looking for.

Walking Without Pulling—Level 3

1. Follow the steps in Level 2. Begin introducing other dogs and people to the environment. If she's distracted, interrupt her with a sound such as "uh-oh," "ooops," or "nope" and a motion such as waving your hand in front of her face—if necessary, with food in your hand. Put other people and dogs at a distance where she'll successfully follow your cue.

2. Gradually decrease the distance between you and the distraction until she'll respond even with another dog or another person right next to her.

Walking Without Pulling—Level 4

In Level 4 you will be adding even more distance and distractions so your dog will walk without pulling wherever and whenever you ask.

1. Add more distractions while asking your dog to walk without pulling. Start training at a distance where your dog is successful. Gradually build up the distractions to include loud and sudden noises, such as noisy traffic, banging pots, dropping chairs, whistling, people wearing floppy coats, and bouncing basketballs.

Practice at the veterinarian's office, the homes of neighbors and relatives, inside the pet store, and at carnivals. Practice hand signals only and then practice voice signals only.

As vigilant as we are in trying not to jerk our dogs or put them in the position of jerking themselves, there are times when your dog will simply bolt. In emergencies, you've got to stop him for safety purposes. This is another good reason to use the Sof-Touch leash to minimize the chances of your dog hurting himself.

If your dog does bolt, however, and you know he's going to come to the end of the leash, quickly—before he hits the end—shout "stop" or "stay." The next thing he'll notice is that this warning came immediately before he reached the end of the leash and was forced to stop. Then get his attention and, in a positive, happy way, lead him elsewhere, away from the distraction. Let me repeat, I am totally against jerking a dog or allowing him to jerk himself. Please do everything you can to create situations where that doesn't happen. In this extreme situation, when an accident does occur, the exercise of yelling "stop" will be very effective and it's better than not doing anything.

Stop

There's a term in animal training called stimulus control. It basically means your dog will reliably do what you ask virtually every time in every situation. In other words, sit means sit wherever and whenever. As mentioned before, in most cases 80 percent reliability is considered good. To train your dog to 90 percent reliability takes a big commitment of time and energy. For this reason, most people aren't really interested in getting to this level of stimulus control with their dogs. There's no such thing as 100 percent reliability with dogs. However, even if you aren't able to invest the time and energy for such control with most behaviors, I suggest you take the time to train your dog to a reliable level for the "stop" behavior. In case of emergency, it might save her life or keep her from another danger, such as being sprayed by a skunk.

When they hear a particular underwater sound, whales and dolphins at water parks are trained to stop whatever they are doing and go to their pens. Water park trainers have a terrific sense of potential problems. If a dangerous situation is even hinted at, the buzzer sounds and all of the marine mammals swim to their respective pens. This illustrates stimulus control for that particular behavior. When you teach your dog "stop," you are assured that he will freeze in his tracks when you ask him to no matter what he is doing—running out in the street, chasing a squirrel, jumping on the mail carrier, whatever.

Stop is taught in steps, like everything else.

Stop—Level 1

The first level of stop is to teach your dog to stop by your side.

1. Start walking with your dog by your side.
2. Take a few steps and put your left palm in front of your dog's nose as you come to a stop. This is the same hand signal for stay. Say "stop" immediately preceding the hand signal; then click and treat.
3. Then, walk with your dog and say "stop"; signal with your hand and leave it there but take *an extra step past your dog*. (See Illustration 38.)
4. Repeat numerous times and progress to two steps past your dog.
5. By now she's getting it. Now say "stop" and omit the hand signal. Walk five steps ahead. Always return to your dog, click, treat, and praise. (Then continue to increase the distance—six steps, seven steps, and so on.)

Stop—Level 2

At Level 2, you are ready to teach your dog to stop from in front of you.

1. Have your dog sit and then walk about 6 feet away from her.
2. Call her and when she gets halfway to you, move your right foot forward. As you're stepping toward her, shoot your right palm toward her also and say "stop." Click and treat.
3. Repeat a thousand times.
4. Gradually add distance. Vary your distance from her when you ask her to stop.

Stop—Level 3

Now your dog is ready to learn to stop from behind. This is a tricky stage but if you've dotted your i's and crossed your t's in the first two levels, your dog will respond to this level too. Most times when you're out for a walk, your dog is—with your permission, of course—out ahead of you. From now on include "stop" as part of your morning and evening walks. Make sure the leash is slack when you do this. Remember, there's no jerking here.

1. Say "stop." Click, praise, and walk up to your dog and reward her with treats when she stops. She has already learned to stay still in the context of having you by her side and in front of her. Now she should automatically stop in this context as well, as long as there are no distractions.
2. Repeat over many sessions at various distances.

Note: Remember, if this doesn't work, back up to the level where your dog is successful.

Stop—Level 4

You've now reached an advanced level of stop. At this level of training, you will be upping the ante in terms of both distance and distractions. Each one has to be practiced individually, though they often overlap.

1. On your walks, add distance by extending the space between you and your dog until you can get her to stop 50 to 100 feet in front of you.
2. Now add some distractions. Ask your neighbor or a family member to volunteer some help by approaching you and your dog from a distance of 50 feet. Your dog should be within 6 feet of you. Estimate the distance you think your dog will successfully respond to your "stop."
3. As your neighbor approaches, say "stop" at the predetermined distance. Click, praise, and treat. Gradually progress to the point where your dog will stop inches away from your neighbor.

4. Now add another distraction. Go back to the original distance of 6 feet from your dog and ask your approaching neighbor to call your dog. As your dog gets halfway to her, say "stop." If your dog stops, click, treat, and praise. If not, say "oops," lead her back to you and try again. Most dogs will get it by the third try. Slowly extend the distance between you and your dog. The variable here is that you are overriding your neighbor's signal. Repeat over and over.

5. Now start the whole process over, this time adding your neighbor's dog as another distraction. When you're successful after thousands of repetitions, go to Level 5.

Stop—Level 5

Now you're on a roll. As a matter of fact, Level 5 includes rolling. To reach this level, your dog has successfully stopped more than three thousand times over a period of several months. Many dogs take up to a year to get to the level of reliability we're talking about here. Of course, it all depends on your commitment, your dog's age, and so on. This behavior is similar to Level 4 of Come When Called.

1. Stand behind your dog and roll a ball past her and tell her to stop. Click and treat.
2. Roll the ball faster, say "stop," click, and treat.
3. Each of these steps is repeated dozens if not hundreds and thousands of times, spread out over many sessions.
4. Now get a motorized mouse. These toys are often advertised in pet magazines. They are actually sold as cat toys, but just keep that fact a secret from your dog. Roll the motorized mouse past your dog, say "go get it" and, just as she gets going, say "stop." Click and treat. This is a huge test. If your dog is successful here, you've just about got it. If not, go back a step or two and work on that behavior.
5. The final step is to take your dog to a park with squirrels and rabbits and do the exercise in that environment. If you can do this, you should be writing your own training book.

ILLUSTRATION 38

At Level 1 take a few steps and put your palm in front of your dog's nose as you come to a stop. Progress by having her stop while you keep walking farther and farther away.

ILLUSTRATION 39

At Level 2, face your dog from a distance of about 6 feet. Call her to you. Step toward her and shoot your palm in front of her and say "stop."

ILLUSTRATION 40

At Level 3, stand behind your dog. Send her forward a few steps and then say "stop." Remember to click, praise, and reward after each repetition. Gradually progress to have her taking more and more steps away from you at a faster and faster speed.

Take It and Drop It

As I've mentioned earlier, my dog Molly and I do a program in elementary schools called *Nonviolence Works!*, in which we illustrate the ways in which the principles of kindness, respect, and responsibility are linked to the way we treat dogs and each other. The highlight of our visits is when the children tell Molly to "answer the phone." She answers the phone by picking the receiver up in her mouth and then, on cue, when I tell her it's a bill collector, she ceremoniously dumps it in a wastebasket. Molly learned to "answer the phone" using this take it and drop it behavior. Service dogs do a lot of "take it and drop it" when they help disabled people by picking up objects, answering the phone, opening doors, and so on.

There are several methods you can use to teach this behavior. In fact, a whole chapter could be written on the various ways to do this. However, the following method is as good as any and better than most.

Take It and Drop It—Level 1

In Level 1, you'll teach the "take it" part of take it and drop it.

1. Rub a piece of turkey on the object you want your dog to take.
2. Put it on the floor. As you do this, say "take it." As your dog examines the object and touches it with his nose, click, praise, and treat with a $10,000 treat.
3. Pick up the object and repeat steps 1 and 2 many times.
4. Now wait until your dog licks the object. When he does, click, praise, and treat. Repeat many times. (Don't reward if he simply touches it with his nose.)
5. Now wait for your dog to touch the object with his mouth and actually pick it up with his mouth, if only for a second. Lavishly praise this behavior, click, and treat.
6. Now put the object in your hand and ask your dog to take it from you and hold onto it for longer and longer periods of time, rewarding each subsequent success.
7. Finally, throw the object away from you and ask your dog to retrieve it.

You can hurry this whole process along by using the words "take it" at other times during the day. For example, take a $10,000 treat and throw it off to the side as you say "take it." Repeat these steps over and over again. Your dog will quickly associate the words with something orally terrific.

Some dogs pick up this behavior extremely quickly. This is especially true of retrievers. So it's a good example of knowing your dog's learning baseline. (See Learning Baseline on page 139.) Always start at the point where your dog is successful and build from there.

Take It and Drop It—Level 2

Now you're ready for the "drop it" part of take it and drop it.

1. Once your dog is reliably taking the object, present a $10,000 treat *or* an object that is identical to the one he is holding in his mouth.

2. Say "drop it" and reward your dog when the object falls from his mouth.
3. The reward can either be the treat or you can throw the identical object, like a second tennis ball, as the reward. This works great because now you have one behavior, the retrieve, acting as a reward for another, the "drop it."

It can be easier to teach your dog "take it and drop it" if you see someone else teach it. For that reason, I suggest enrolling in a class or getting a video.

Emergency "Drop It"

If you have to open your dog's mouth in an emergency situation, gently roll his skin over his teeth. You can do this by grabbing the bottom or the top of the dog's muzzle. Most dogs will open their mouths when they feel the skin on their teeth. Say "drop it" while you are doing this and reward your dog even though he was forced to let it go. (Do not hurt your dog.)

Congratulations! You've read a lot. Treat yourself to a movie or read a great book like *Replay* by Ken Grimwood.

PART III

Dealing with Problem Behaviors

Causes of Problem Behaviors

Remember, from a dog's perspective there is no such thing as a problem behavior. He's doing what he's doing for a reason. And, to look at it from another perspective, a behavior *you* don't consider a problem might be one to other people. You might like your dog jumping on you when you get home but others don't. If your dog's behavior is harmful to him, the environment, other people, other animals, or you, it deserves immediate attention.

Physiological and neurological problems can impact your dog's behavior. Therefore, before implementing any behavioral modification program, ask your veterinarian to do a thorough exam. If health problems exist, work closely with your veterinarian and/or a professional trainer who uses nonviolent training methods.

Basil, a three-year-old male German shepherd, got off the family sofa and walked toward her handler, April, as she was teaching her year-old baby girl to walk. Without hesitating, Basil walked around April and suddenly bit the baby in the face. I got the call the same day. The dog was now locked in his kennel and April was in tears, wondering if there was anything she could do so her baby would be safe with Basil around. Would Basil always be a threat to children? Would it be necessary to have him euthanized?

On investigation, I learned there were several factors that contributed to Basil's behavior. First, there was an obvious lack of training—Basil had never been taught what was expected of him when the baby was in the room. In addition, the veterinarian found

Basil was developing an arthritic condition and therefore was probably in some pain. And, finally, Basil may have been protecting his toy, which April later found hidden under the couch.

This story illustrates the severe problems that can develop when one or more of the nine ingredients are imbalanced or missing in your dog's life. In Basil's case, he had not been provided with *sufficient* play, socialization, exercise, employment, or positive reinforcement training. Basil was being himself, a dog that was behaving with the hand that he was dealt. He viewed himself as head of the house and was willing to assert his authority, guarding his territory and his possessions.

Fortunately, there was a happy ending to this story and, with a watchful eye and resolute commitment by the family, Basil is growing old alongside them. The baby sustained only superficial cuts that healed quickly and there were no scars.

In most cases problem behaviors are caused by an imbalance in the nine ingredients. (Exceptions are those cases where physical or neurological influences are involved.) Let's look at some of the ways these imbalances could be occurring:

High Quality Diet: Is your dog chewing things or misbehaving because of hunger? Or is his diet low in essential nutrients? Sometimes a dog chews on objects because the body, in its own wisdom, is seeking nutrients that are missing or underprovided in the diet. For instance, if your dog chews on grass, eats feces, or eats from a cat's litter box, his body may be looking for missing nutrients. While a little bit of grass can be okay, it can be problematic if the lawn has been sprayed with pesticides or if chemical fertilizers have been used. Is your dog "hyper" because of all the salt and sugar he's being fed due to a low quality pet food? Is he having problems "holding it" while in the house? Maybe he's been drinking more water than usual because of too much salt in the rawhide bones and other chewies he's been fed.

Play, Exercise, and Socialization: Many dogs are simply bored and frustrated because they're not getting enough physical, emotional, and mental stimulation. They don't get enough exercise. They don't get to socialize with their dog pals and other human beings. They are bored because they haven't been presented with anything new and exciting lately.

🦴 *Employment:* Does your dog have a "job" to do? If you don't provide an environment for him to express himself, he'll chew, or bark, or jump just to keep himself "employed."

🦴 *Rest:* Is your dog getting enough rest? Many problem behaviors, including snapping or growling, can manifest because your dog is exhausted.

🦴 *Training:* Some people think their dogs are stubborn or dumb but many dogs are simply confused because they haven't been trained in different situations or they're confused because they haven't successfully repeated the behavior you're asking for enough times. (Review Context Learning in Chapter 6 on page 89.)

🦴 *Quiet Time:* Does your dog have a place to "get away from it all" for quality quiet time? Maybe his jumping and chewing are simply stress relievers.

🦴 *Health Care:* Does your dog have a physical problem that might be contributing to the chewing problem?

Unintentional Training

As well intentioned and diligent as you might be during your dog's training process, certain situations may crop up in which his behavior is the opposite of what you intended. In many cases, you are directly responsible for eliciting the problem behavior in the first place.

Let's say you want to calm your nervous dog that is shaking and pacing from the sound of fireworks on the Fourth of July or the lightning and thunder from a summer storm. When the fireworks start to blast or the thunder rumbles, you might soothe your dog by stroking him and murmuring, "It's okay, Benjie. Everything's fine. Gooooood dog." In these cases, you may be inadvertently practicing unintentional training because your dog views the praise as a reward for the behavior. In other words, you are actually rewarding behavior you are trying to discourage.

Or let's say you are talking on the phone and your dog starts barking for attention. A normal response is to interrupt the call and yell at the dog, *"Be quiet!"* Once again, you may be rewarding the undesirable behavior. In this case, you are giving your dog what he wants—your attention.

Remember the rules of reinforcement—your dog's behavior can be increased or decreased by your response to that behavior. In other words, in these examples listed, your actions could actually be reinforcing the behavior you want him to stop. Telling a dog "It's okay" while he's shivering because of the fireworks or thunder may actually be reinforcing the nervousness! Giving your dog attention, whether positive or negative, while he is barking for attention, may actually reinforce the barking. The trick is to stop *reacting* and remember to *respond* instead. (See Responding Versus Reacting to Your Dog on page 10.)

When considering what do to with your dog's "problem" behavior, try to look at the situation from your dog's point of view. Take a mental snapshot of the environment at the time of the problem behavior. Become aware of what your dog is actually learning from the people and events around him. Changing the environment is the most important consideration. I will share specific ways to handle each of the behavioral problems addressed in this chapter. In general, though, in order to modify your dog's behavior, it's helpful to begin by reviewing the following steps.

To respond to any undesirable behavior, follow these steps:

1. Take a step back from the situation and pause (unless you, the dog, or the environment is in danger).
2. Do a round of three complete breaths (see page 65).
3. Ask yourself, "What do I want my dog *to do?"* rather than "What do I want my dog *to stop* doing?" Write down your goals.
4. Review the 8 Tools of Dog Training in Chapter 7 and pick one or two or three that you think would work for the situation.
5. Make an outline, plan the steps you are going to take, and create the environment necessary to implement your plan.
6. Practice.
7. Review the results and amend your actions as necessary. If you're not sure how to proceed, a private class with a nonviolent dog trainer may be necessary.

> **Aggressive Behavior**
> If your dog exhibits aggressive behavior, it's important that you consult a behavioral specialist and be willing to spend the time necessary to resolve the problem by overhauling your own daily routine. Aggression should be taken seriously and handled right away. The ramifications are serious, ranging from injury to financial liabilities. Aggression and other serious behavioral problems are beyond the scope of this book.

How to Handle Problem Behaviors

The Behavioral Building Blocks chart on page 119 will give you a broader landscape of the possible reasons for a behavior problem and how to deal with it. In the example given in this chart, I'm using barking as a problem behavior. However, any problem behavior will fit in this model. The chart offers a small sampling of the reasons a dog could be barking. The truth of the matter is, unless there is a physiological or neurological problem, the dog is probably barking because (1) he wants to express himself because he's excited or nervous, and (2) you haven't given him any reason to do otherwise, such as rewarding him for being quiet. Some dogs bark for hours on end; it almost seems as if they are barking just to hear themselves bark.

To obtain a "quiet" behavior, you have to follow the rules. (See Barking on page 204.) Start training at your dog's learning baseline (see page 139) and gradually build from there. Go through the steps on the chart and determine the source of the problem. First of all, what is triggering your dog's behavior? A squirrel in the tree, another dog in the yard, a mail carrier walking toward your house? Then, which of the nine ingredients are lacking or out of balance and helped to shape this behavior in the first place.

Let's say you determine that your dog is barking due to (1) a general lack of socialization; (2) boredom due to a general lack of structured play time; and/or (3) a territorial guarding impulse. Now look at the suggestions for dealing with barking on the Behavioral Building Blocks chart on page 119. Put one or more of these suggestions on your

Daily Routines Sheet (see page 50) and hang it on the refrigerator to help you remember what to do. The key is to keep it simple by adding some of these elements to your regular lifestyle, rather than writing down more than you can realistically accomplish.

Before you begin working on any problem behavior: Review each of the *nine ingredients* in Chapter 2 to be sure that, along with training, you are providing proper amounts and quality of food, play, socialization, quiet time, exercise, mental stimulation (employment), rest, and health care.

Barking

When your dog barks:

1. Ignore it. Many behaviors simply disappear when they are not reinforced.
2. Distract your dog with sound or movement and then give a "quiet" signal. (See Quiet on page 179.)
3. Get up and walk around. Reward your dog when she pays attention or goes into a heeling position.
4. Desensitize your dog to the stimulus that is prompting him to bark by moving him farther away from it and/or decreasing the intensity of the stimulus. For example, if your dog is barking at another dog, move the other dog away from your dog. Then, over time, gradually move closer to the other dog.
5. Make sure your dog has eliminated. Maybe your dog is over his stress threshold. If he needs to eliminate but hasn't had the opportunity, that is yet one more stress. Lightening his stress load in this way might help him move more comfortably and also deal better with other stresses.
6. Block the view of your dog.
7. Put some peanut butter or caramel on the roof of your dog's mouth.
8. Hold your dog firmly but gently until quiet. Release when his muscles relax, even slightly. Say "okay," or another release word.

Begging at the Table

1. Ignore the begging.
2. Tether or kennel your dog and play the magnet game (page 159). Whenever she sits or lies down, throw her a treat or get up to pet her.
3. Distract your dog with sound or motion and ask her to go to her spot. Once she has the basic "go to your spot" behavior down, gradually progress to the point where you send her to her spot while you are actually sitting at the table. Then progress to having her lie down and stay on that spot throughout your dinnertime. (See Go to Your Spot on page 170.)
4. Use a chew toy or a smart toy to keep her busy. (See Toys on page 34.)

Behaving in a Shy or Fearful Manner

1. Use a calm, gentle voice and slow movements.
2. Ignore the behavior and let the pooch explore when ready. Ignore submissive behaviors and reward more social behaviors.
3. Approximating is key. Begin at the lowest level of acceptance and build from there. (See the Handling Baseline Chart on page 145.)
4. Allow a shy dog to win a game of tug of war.
5. Allow plenty of room between dogs and consider differences in sex, size, and temperament.
6. Use social facilitation by putting another dog in the shy dog's vicinity and letting them interact.
7. Make environmental changes in the home. Feed twice a day to help remove the stress of hunger and put the dog's sleeping quarters in the handler's bedroom for bonding. If the dog has the run of the house when handlers are gone, she may feel her job of protecting the entire house is too stressful. To avoid this, lessen the roaming area while working on separation anxiety. Make sure the dog has a "safe spot" for security. The list of changes you can make to the environment is endless. Your instructor can make further recommendations for your dog in a private class.

8. Avoid eye contact with the dog at first and slowly work for the dog's attention.
9. Introduce "smart" toys that promote confidence, such as the Buster Cube, Kong, and treat balls.
10. Introduce agility games to improve confidence.

Chewing

When dealing with any problem behavior the first thing to do is review the nine ingredients (Chapter 2) and determine how you can upgrade and balance them. With the chewing behavior, this is especially evident. Dogs chew furniture, holes in walls, wires, sticks, clothes, and virtually everything else. Teaching your dog what to chew on and where to chew it is practical in terms of keeping your belongings and home in order, as well as promoting your dog's safety.

Here are some tips to help with the chewing problem:

1. Schedule two 15- to 30-minute quality-with-doggie times a day to play, exercise, and socialize your dog. A dog that is stimulated is less likely to vent his boredom and frustration in ways that create problems for his human family. Run with your dog and play fetch, hide-and-seek, and find it. Train him to sit, lie down, stand, stay, and come when called. Teach him tricks such as sit up, roll over, play dead, and answer the phone.
2. Give your dog "legal" chew toys such as the Nyla, Gumma, or Booda bones and a smart toy, such as a Kong, Buster Cube, or a plastic treat ball.
3. Teach "leave it": Put several objects in the middle of the floor. Watch for your dog to check them out for "chewability." Interrupt him while he's thinking about it with the words, "leave it," and then click, praise, and reward with a legal chewy.
4. Above all, practice prevention by creating an environment where your dog can be successful. Remove illegal objects so your dog can't get to them in the first place and use management methods such as tethering, baby gates, and a kennel so your dog is not tempted to chew on the wrong items.

Eliminating in the House

It's important to follow a strict set of rules when teaching a puppy to eliminate where and when you want.

1. Set a schedule. Puppies up to about 3 months of age need to eliminate 8 to 10 times a day. Scheduled times should include:

   🦴 *First thing in the morning when you get up*

   🦴 *15 to 30 minutes after eating (3 meals per day)*

   🦴 *After play or other excitement*

   🦴 *When you get home from work or school*

   🦴 *Early evening*

   🦴 *Just before bed*

   🦴 *During the night (if necessary)*

2. Always take the puppy to the same location to eliminate.
3. Mark or label the elimination behavior with a word. For instance, encourage him with a friendly voice saying "hurry up" or "outside" or "go potty." As soon as your dog finishes, praise and reward him with a treat.
4. Manage your environment. Keep your dog in a kennel or tethered so she can't make mistakes. If you tether her, make sure it's in a social area. Never leave a dog tethered alone. You can tether her to you by attaching her leash to your waist. The late trainer Job Michael Evans called this an "umbilical cord," which is a nice metaphor.
5. Keep the elimination time envelope short. Give your dog ten minutes to "go." If she doesn't eliminate within the ten-minute time frame, bring her back in the house and put her in her kennel or tether her. Try it again fifteen minutes later.
6. Remember the one-second rule. If you walk in the room three seconds after your dog has peed on the carpet, she won't associate a reprimand with the behavior. So don't reprimand her at all. If you catch her in the act, startle her with excitement but don't scare her. Shout "Oh, my gosh" and run to her. The idea is to have her stop what she's doing without freaking her out. Pick her up or head her

outside all the while shouting, "Oh, my. Oh, my." As soon as you get outside, act thoroughly relieved. Relax your voice and body. Then encourage her with "go outside" or "hurry up."

7. Don't give your dog any food or water after eight o'clock in the evening. Leave a couple of ice cubes for her.

8. Although some puppies can "hold it" all through the night as young as eight weeks, many need to eliminate during the night so you'll have to set your alarm to take her out. The elimination needs of each individual puppy will vary; however, here are some guidelines for puppies eight weeks and older: If the dog is younger than three months old, take her out every 4 to 5 hours. This means if you go to bed at 10:00 P.M., get up at 2:00 or 3:00 A.M. and take her out again. Keep adding 15-minute increments every 2 or 3 days until you're confident she can make it for 7 to 8 hours. Most dogs can "hold it" overnight once they reach four months of age. You'll know you've gone too fast if you find she's eliminated in her kennel or pen area.

Note: *If you bring your dog in the house after she eliminates and then immediately leave for the day, your dog will quickly learn that eliminating is associated with your leaving. As a result, she'll start procrastinating while she's outside. Instead, once you're back in the house, let her spend five to ten minutes playing with you or a chew toy before you leave.*

When your dog eliminates in the house:

🦴 Clean up the urine with a nonammoniated cleanser. There are several on the market.

🦴 Don't let her see you clean it up. There's still a debate about this, but some behaviorists think you might be giving your dog a message that you're accepting her little "gifts."

> **TIP** Once a day put a few pieces of kibble on a paper plate and place it on any spot where your dog has previously eliminated in the house. Dogs hate to eliminate where they eat.

Grabbing the Leash While Heeling

1. Teach your dog to "go get the leash" before every walk. Sometimes a dog will learn not to put the leash in her mouth unless she knows it's associated with a walk.
2. Teach your dog free heeling using a target stick before teaching her to heel on a leash. (See Targeting on page 108 and Heeling on page 183.)
3. If she's looking at you, then she's not chewing on the leash, so practice more *"pay attention"* exercises. (See Pay Attention on page 152.)
4. Teach your dog to release the leash on command. (See Take It and Drop It on page 193.)
5. Anticipate the undesirable behavior of chewing the leash while walking before it happens; distract your dog, and train him for another behavioral response, such as heel or sit.
6. Use a halter-style collar.
7. Soak the leash in bitter apple or Listerine mouthwash. If neither or those work, try bitter orange. (Bitter apple can be purchased in pet supply stores; bitter orange must be prescribed by your veterinarian.)

Jumping on People

When your dog jumps on a person:

1. Turn away from your dog and give her no attention.
2. Interrupt your dog from even thinking about jumping by interjecting some sound or motion and then put her in the sit or down position before the jumping occurs.
3. When at home, lower the greeting effect when leaving and returning. Simply say a soft "hello" when you come home and

"later" or "see ya" when you depart. Don't act excited. Praise and pet your dog only when she is sitting or lying down or generally more relaxed.

4. Give him something else to do whenever you walk into the room like going to his bed. (This behavior can then be linked to the cue of you entering the room.)

5. Just before the dog reaches you, throw a treat to the side, saying "take it." Then have the dog return and sit.

6. Teach your dog to jump on signal. In other words, have her sit, *then* have her jump up on you as a reward for sitting.

7. Gently hold her paws and release moments after she wants to be released.

Lunging Aggressively at Other Dogs

Of all the behavior problems listed, this one most often reflects how you are feeling and what you are communicating to your dog. Many dogs are taught to be aggressive because the person at the other end of the leash is anxious and communicates that anxiety to the dog. In essence, you're saying, "That approaching dog or person is a threat. Protect me!" If this is the case, change your attitude first, then change your dog's behavior.

A number of suggestions are offered here; however, a professional trainer is required to deal with aggressive behavior. Be sure you find a trainer who uses nonviolent methods.

1. Management is a key to handling this problem. A halter-style collar will help.

2. Hold the dog in such a way as to not be pulled off balance. Do this by keeping your elbows bent and your arms close to your body. Keep your knees slightly bent and balance your weight.

3. Have another dog walk by at a distance that does not bother the aggressive dog as much and be ready to reward your dog for moments of quiet behavior. Repeat. As the other dog walks closer, ask your dog to pay attention to you and reward her when she does. (See Pay Attention on page 152.) Repeat this exercise, slowly decreasing the distance between the dogs.

4. Stop the lunging behavior before it happens by distracting your dog with a sound or motion while she's thinking about it.
5. Whenever another dog comes by, use William Campbell's Jolly Routine as outlined in training tool number 6, change the association. (See page 116.)
6. Find a less threatening dog and reward him first, then give the aggressive dog a reward. Repeat this over and over by touching the other dog and throwing your dog a treat. Eventually the aggressive dog will begin to look at the other dog in a positive way.
7. Continue practicing behaviors such as sit and stay, progressing to advanced levels. When your dog is so focused on you, the aggressive behavior diminishes as she relinquishes control to you.

Note: Spay or neuter your dog. Lunging at other dogs is often reduced when your dog is spayed or neutered. An intact male dog is three times more likely to attack than a neutered dog. A spayed female will not have the same maternal protectiveness and is also less likely to mouth or nip. Because she doesn't have to protect her young, she doesn't have to protect the territory around her.

Mouthing or Nipping Handler

Try a number of these methods. Do two or three repetitions of one method, then alternate with another.

1. Practice "ouch" training. When you feel so much as a tooth for whatever reason, immediately make a sound like a puppy yelping, like the word "yipe." This holds true whether it's a playful puppy nipping at you or an older dog mouthing your arm. When you make this sound, most dogs and puppies will immediately back off. When your dog does back off, give praise. *Note: If your dog gets more excited when you do this, this is not the technique for him. Don't do it.*
2. Use the "aaaah!" method. Lower your vocal pitch and interrupt the mouthing with a quick "aaaah." To some dogs this is perceived as a low-intensity growl. We use it simply as an interrupter—to

interrupt the behavior. *Note: If your dog gets more excited when you do this, this is not the technique for him. Don't do it.*

3. Give a "yipe" or "aaaah" and then leave the room or put the puppy or dog in a two- to five-minute time out. A good way to handle the time out is to put him behind a baby gate. Then, after the time is up, return his freedom and let him know that everything between you is now okay and there are no hard feelings. The combination of making a sound and giving a time out is very powerful.

4. Before your dog has a chance to chew on you, give him something legal to chew on like a Booda or Nyla bone. Or give him a treat-filled Kong to play with.

5. Before your teething puppy has a chance to mouth or nip you, give him an ice cube or a piece of frozen canvas. Or put one of the aforementioned bone toys in the freezer for 10 minutes or so and then give it to him. This helps numb the gums for a while, alleviating the discomfort of emerging teeth.

6. Put the puppy on the floor whenever a nip occurs and walk away.

7. Teach the dog to lick on signal instead of nipping you. Rub some turkey, peanut butter, or cream cheese on your hand. As your puppy licks it off, say "lick." Then click, praise, and treat with turkey. Another variation of this tip is to simply lick the palm of your hand and then let your dog lick your saliva.

8. Ignore the dog's biting, but praise everything else.

9. Put the dog's kennel in a social area or tether him so nipping can't occur. Reward calm behavior.

10. Immediately hold the dog gently but firmly until her body relaxes. Then say "okay" and release. (See Illustration 37 on page 182.)

11. Practice the management methods in Chapter 9 and use a halter-style collar.

12. If the dog is nipping ankles or feet, have her sit or lie down when you are approaching and/or use a leash tied around your waist to lead the dog away from your feet.

13. Ask your veterinarian if it's okay to give a teething pup one-quarter of an aspirin before class to reduce inflammation and soreness of gums.

Running Away

Until your dog is so trained that she awaits your every request, you must take extra precautions so she can't run away. Safety is paramount. You must be able to manage your dog and your environment. Therefore, unless your dog is in an enclosed area, never let him off the leash.

The key to avoiding problems is to anticipate them. If you see another dog, a squirrel, or a cat, you can bet your dog is going to want to say hello. When you catch your dog even *thinking* about it, give her something else to do, like asking her to sit, lie down, heel, and so on.

Keep Your Dog from Running Out When You Open the Door

Practice the following "door fan" method to keep Fido from running out when you leave.

1. Say nothing. Then open the door 2 inches and let Fido think he's going out. When the door doesn't open all the way, he'll back off and perhaps walk around a little. As he backs off, open the door wider. He'll scoot back, ready to bolt, but as he moves toward the door again, quickly close it back to the 2-inch mark. Repeat over and over until your dog sits. Then say "okay" and open the door wide. (Keep your dog on a long leash if the yard is not enclosed.) Please be careful not to catch your dog's nose in the door!

2. Progress to opening the door but telling him to stay. Go through the door first, then say "okay."

3. Once outside, progress to having him come and stay by you for a second or two.

Separation Anxiety

Dogs are social animals. Remember the story I related in Chapter 1 about Raju, the puppy of my neighbors in India? This little social animal was separated from his pack. He was in a new environment that was really scary, because of all the new sights and sounds. Plus, he was tied up. Dogs have an inbred resistance to being restrained. In short, Raju's stress threshold was crossed and, among other things, he was suffering from separation anxiety.

Signs of Separation Anxiety

🦴 Whining, whimpering, and barking (vocal manifestations);

🦴 Urinating and defecating, runny nose, panting, and sweaty paws (visceral manifestations);

🦴 Pacing, shivering, jumping, clawing, digging, and crashing through windows (somatic manifestations); and/or

🦴 Chewing the furniture or other objects, ripping up the linoleum, or chewing himself (oral manifestations).

If your dog exhibits signs of separation anxiety, the first thing to do is to create a safe environment. Make sure there's nothing your dog can chew on or destroy. If necessary, segregate her in a pen or in the kitchen, using baby gates as barriers in doorways. These options won't work for some dogs, especially rescue dogs with a past history of negligence. In those cases, a kennel is mandatory. I know of several dogs who have crashed through safety glass windows trying to get out of a house. One dog, a huge mastiff, did this from the second story. In these extreme circumstances, it's mandatory for someone to take a week off from work to work with the dog and teach him to enjoy the kennel. (See Go to Your Spot on page 170.) (Separation anxiety is directly and powerfully affected by reviewing, integrating, and balancing the nine ingredients given in Chapter 2!)

Here are a few more tips to deal with separation anxiety:
1. *Lower your energy level when you depart and arrive.* A simple "see ya" when you leave and ignoring her until she settles down when you get home will do wonders. She'll feed off your calmness and security. In essence, you're telling her being separated is no big deal. In addition, if she remains calm, she gets rewarded.
2. *Set a schedule.* Dogs thrive on routines. Once they know when you're going and coming, they relax more because they are able to predict the future.
3. *Give a special toy or treats.* Just before you leave, give her a special toy such as a treat-filled Kong, Buster Cube, or other treat ball. Give this particular special toy *only* when you leave.

Eventually your dog will look forward to you going out the door. Alternatively, hide a dozen treats around the kitchen. As you're leaving tell your dog to "stay" and then, as you walk out the door, say "find it."

4. *Turn on a radio or television.* Choose a channel that you normally listen to. Soothing classical or New Age music, such as Steven Halpern's "Inner Peace Music" series, is best. In fact, I'd suggest that you turn it on as soon as you awaken and leave it on when you leave. That way your dog will associate this music with you being around.

5. *Implement "depart" and "return" sessions.*
   a. Say "see ya," open the door, close it, click, and treat.
   b. Say "see ya," open the door, go through it without closing it, return, click, and treat.
   c. Say "see ya," open the door, go through it, close the door, silently count "one thousand one," open the door, and click and treat.

   For advanced depart and return:

   🦴 Continue the depart and return routine, adding one second each time, until you reach a ten-second wait outside the door for the first session. Do three to five sessions during the day.

   🦴 As your dog progresses, add distance. Take two steps away from the door while you are outside, then come back in, click, and treat. Gradually add more distance, taking three steps, four steps, and so on.

   🦴 Within a few days, go outside, get in your car, and close the door. After one second, get out of the car, come back in the house, click, and reward. Repeat this for at least one session. Then proceed to doing the entire process over again but this time start the car and then turn it off and return to the house. Repeat one full session. The next time, repeat the process but this time back down the driveway, pull back in, and enter the house. Click and treat. You get the idea. Progress at your dog's speed.

Some severe cases of separation anxiety require all of these steps and more. If your dog is less anxious, you may not need to do any of the steps except the one in which you get into your car.

6. *Herbs, flower essences, aromatherapy, and homeopathic remedies.* Holistic veterinarians recommend natural alternatives such as herbs, flower essences (such as Bach Flower Remedies), aromatherapy, and homeopathic remedies to help deal with separation anxiety and other emotionally based issues. I have included several distributors of products in these categories in Appendix C. If your dog has a separation anxiety problem, you can learn more about incorporating a natural remedy in his treatment program from a veterinarian who is holistically oriented. You can also consult other books including *The Natural Dog,* by Mary Brennan, D.V.M., *Beyond Obedience,* by April Frost, and *Four Paws, Five Directions,* by Cheryl Schwartz, D.V.M.

7. *Medication.* There are several pharmaceutical drugs that are used in conjunction with behavior modification programs for separation anxiety, as well as other behaviors. Contact a behaviorist who uses nonviolence methodology and your veterinarian if you want to look into pharmaceutical alternatives.

8. *Confidence building.* Building a dog's confidence builds a sense of security. Although it's recommended that you stay home to help a new canine family member make his transition to new surroundings, it's equally important to loosen his "neediness." In other words, you need to show him that being alone is okay too. Your dog will gain confidence and security through the use of smart toys, the find it game on page 168, and the depart and return routine given in suggestion 5 in this list. Emotional health is also encouraged and promoted through advanced training in sit and lie down, such as increasing your distance from your dog and going out of your dog's sight while you are training for these behaviors. These behaviors should initially be taught indoors, then progress to teaching them outdoors. In addition, I highly recommend enrolling in socialization classes and agility, herding, water work, and/or tracking

classes, depending on your dog's sensitivity level. In these classes, other handlers will work with your dog and you will work with other dogs. Distance and out-of-sight training exercises are also practiced. All of these behaviors and activities communicate to your dog that everything's okay and that he can adapt and be safe.

9. *Exercise your dog before you leave.* If you get your dog a little tired, he'll have less energy to burn off while you're gone.

appendix a

Nonviolence Works! In Schools

To help promote nonviolence toward animals, I have established a not-for-profit organization, Raise With Praise, Inc., which presents live performances entitled *Nonviolence Works!* in elementary schools. *Nonviolence Works!* instructs children how to deal with animals humanely and how to use these same principles of kindness, respect, and responsibility in their relationships with others. In addition, Raise With Praise, Inc., sponsors after-school programs that are independently evaluated by psychologists to gather data to further establish the link between human-to-animal and human-to-human nonviolence.

For more information, please call or write:

Raise With Praise, Inc.
P.O. Box 10335
Burbank, California 91510
Phone: 800-269-3591
Email: raisewithpraise@webtv.net
Web site: www.raisewithpraise.com

appendix b

Associations and Organizations

Dog Training Associations and Organizations

Association of Pet Dog Trainers, P.O. Box 385, Davis, CA 95617.
  Phone: 800-PET-DOGS; e-mail: apdtbod@aol.com
The National Association of Dog Obedience Instructors,
  729 Grapevine Highway, Suite 369, Hurst, TX 76054-2085.
  Web address: www.kimberly.vidaho.edu/nadoi

For classes in agility, flyball, herding, water work, and tracking, contact professional dog trainers in your area or look for them
on the Internet.

Holistic Veterinary Associations and Organizations

American Holistic Veterinary Medical Association, 2214 Old
  Emmorton Road, Bel Air, MD 21015. Phone: 410-569-0795;
  fax: 410-515-7774. Professional organization that serves as a
  forum to explore alternative veterinary health care. Publishes a
  quarterly journal for members. Send self-addressed stamped
  envelope for list of holistic veterinarians in your area.

American Veterinary Chiropractic Association, P.O. Box 249, Port Byron, IL 61275. Phone: 309-523-3995. Professional organization that promotes veterinary chiropractic.

International Veterinary Acupuncture Society, 2140 Conestoga Road, Chester Springs, PA 19425. Phone: 215-827-7245. Professional organization fosters research on acupuncture in veterinary medicine. Call or write for information and lists of veterinary acupuncturists in the United States and other countries.

National Center for Homeopathy, 801 N. Fairfax, #306, Alexandria, VA 22314. Phone: 703-548-7790. Directory of homeopaths, including veterinarians. Offers a catalog of books and annual courses.

Organizations that Promote Animal-Assisted Therapy

Dogs that are involved in service to people, called service or assistance dogs, have become irreplaceable in the lives of many who are dependent on them in so many ways. Dogs are helping to lead the way in the medical community by using their superlative senses to communicate to us what they detect. For example, they are now being used to predict epileptic seizures, as well as the early stages of cancer, pneumonia, and other diseases that are not yet detectable through high-tech diagnostic machines. What a wonderful partnership! Dogs help the blind see and the deaf hear. They are the hands for those who are unable to reach and the support for those who have difficulty in standing and moving around. In addition, studies have shown that dogs can bolster self-esteem, relieve stress, and promote health and nonviolence.

Delta Society, 289 Perimeter Road East, Renton, WA 98055-1329. Action Phone Line: 800-869-6898; fax: 425-235-1076. An organization founded on the belief that the human-animal bond is inherently important to everyone's health and happiness. Delta Society is dedicated to doing work that furthers this principle and helps to bring all sorts of wonderful creatures together with people. Delta is a place where people with disabilities can find information, guidance, and help for dealing with their situations. Delta also helps train people to become partners with their pets so they both can help others.

Green Chimneys, Putnam Lake Road, Caller Box 719, Brewster, NY 10509-0719. Phone: 914-279-2995; fax: 914-279-2714; Web address: www. pcnet.com/~gchimney. An organization dedicated to providing care and concern for all living things and the development of basic living skills for children and adults in order to strengthen their emotional health and well-being.

The Latham Foundation, Latham Plaza Building, Clement and Schiller Streets, Alameda, CA 94501. Phone: 510-521-0920; fax: 510-521-9861; Web address: www. latham.org. An organization dedicated to "promote, foster, encourage and further the principles of humaneness, kindness and benevolence to all living creatures; the doctrines of universal brotherhood and justice; and the prevention and eradication of cruelty to animals and all living creatures, with particular emphasis on the education of children in justice and kindness to animals."

Humane Societies

American Humane Association, 63 Inverness Drive East, Englewood, CO 80112-5117. Phone: 303-792-9900; Web address: www. royal-components.com. In addition to its many other endeavors on behalf of animals, the American Humane Association operates the National Resource Center on the Link Between Violence to People and Animals.

Humane Society of the United States, 2100 L Street, Washington, D.C. 20037. Phone: 202-293-5100. Among its many programs, the Humane Society of the United States runs a program called First Strike, linking veterinarians, humane societies, and the public in an all-out effort to stop the cycle of violence.

Wisconsin Humane Society, 4151 N. Humboldt Avenue, Milwaukee, WI 53212. Phone: 414-961-0310. The Wisconsin Humane Society operates a program for children called PAL, which stands for People-Animals-Learning. In this outstanding animal-assisted therapy program, at-risk youth learn a newfound respect for animals as they go out into their communities and become humane educators.

Veterinary Behavioral Specialists

American Veterinary Society of Animal Behavior, c/o Laurie Martin, D.V.M., Boughton Square Animal Hospital, 491 W. Boughton, Bolingbrook, Il 60440; email: debhdvm@aol.com. This organization maintains a list of veterinarians with special interests or training in behavior problems.

The American College of Veterinary Behaviorists, Department of Small Animal Medicine and Surgery, College of Veterinary Medicine, Texas A&M University, College Station, TX 77843-4474; Phone: 409-845-2351; email: bbeaver@cvm.tamu.edu. Facilitates education in clinical behavior and certifies training programs for specialists in the field.

appendix c

Product Suppliers

PLEASE NOTE: At the time of this writing, the companies listed supply one or more products that are acceptable within the guidelines of this book. This does not necessarily mean that the authors recommend *all* products made by or sold by these companies.

Product quality can change from year to year; companies can change management or policies or standards. We urge you to keep this in mind, to be continuously alert, and *to read labels* and product brochures carefully, even for products you have been using for a long time.

There may be other fine suppliers or new companies not listed here. The fact that a certain supplier is not listed does not necessarily mean that we wouldn't recommend them if we knew about them.

Mail-Order Catalogs for Books and Videos, Training Gear, and Kennels

Doctors Foster & Smith, 2253 Air Park Road, P.O. Box 100, Rhinelander, WI 54501-0100. Phone: 800-826-7206. General pet supplies.

Dog and Cat Book Catalog, Direct Book Service, P.O. Box 2778, 701B Poplar, Wenatchee, WA 98807-2778. Phone: 800-776-2665; Web address: www.dogandcatbooks.com. Probably the largest and most diverse assortment of dog and cat books and videos anywhere in the world.

In the Company of Dogs, P.O. Box 7071, Dover, DE 19903. Phone: 800-924-5050. Gift items for dog lovers.

J-B Wholesale Pet Supplies, 5 Raritan Road, Oakland, NJ 07436. Phone: 800-526-0388. General pet supplies.

Legacy-by-Mail, P.O. Box 697, Carlsborg, WA 98324. Phone: 888-876-9364; fax: 360-683-5755; Web address: www.legacy-by-mail.com. One of the finest sources of top-of-the-line books and videos. They also sell specialty items such as pouches, leashes, collars, and toys, and other products for dog people from dog people.

Premier Pet Products, 406 Branchway Ct., Richmond, VA 23236. Phone: 800-933-5595; fax: 800-795-5930.

R.C. Steele, P.O. Box 910, Brockport, NY 14420-0910. Phone: 800-872-3773 or 716-637-1408; in Canada: 800-424-2205. General pet supplies.

Mail-Order Catalogs for Natural Products

Jerry Teplitz Enterprises, Inc., 228 N. Donnawood Drive, Suite 204, Virginia Beach, VA 23452. Phone: 800-77-RELAX. Web address: www.teplitz.com. Carries books, music tapes, audiotapes, and other products on stress reduction.

L & H Vitamins, 37-10 Crescent Street, Long Island City, NY 11101. Phone: 800-221-1152. Carries natural supplements, herbs, homeopathics, and Bach Flower Remedies at discounted prices.

Morrill's New Directions, P.O. Box 30, Orient, ME 04471. Phone: 800-368-5057; in Maine, call 800-649-0744. Web address: www.morrills.com. Carries a number of natural pet products we recommend. Free catalog available on request.

The Natural Pet Care Catalog, 8050 Lake City Way, N.E., Seattle, WA 98115. Phone: 800-962-8266 or 206-522-1667; fax: 206-522-1132.

Web address: www.all-the-best.com. Carries natural pet products we recommend. Free catalog available on request.

The Vitamin Shoppe, 4700 Westside Avenue, North Bergen, NJ 07047. Phone: 800-223-1216. Carries vitamins, herbs, homeopathics, and Bach Flower Remedies at discounted prices. Free catalog available on request.

PetSage, 4313 Wheeler Avenue, Alexandria, Virginia 22304; Phone: 703-823-9711; fax: 703-823-9714, Webpage: www.petsage.com. Carries natural products we recommend. Catalog available upon request.

Manufacturers of Natural Pet Foods and Products

Breeder's Choice Pet Foods, Inc., Irwindale, CA 91706; Phone: 800-255-4286. Manufacturers of Pinnacle brand dog food.

Flint River Ranch, 1243 Columbia Avenue, B-6, Riverside, CA 92507. Phone: 909-682-5048; fax: 909-682-5057.

Halo, Purely for Pets, 3438 East Lake Road, Suite 14, Palm Harbor, FL 34685. Phone: 813-854-2214. Web address: www.halopets.com. Manufacturers of Spot's Stew and other natural products including Dream Coat (an oil supplement), Derma Dream (an herbal salve), and Halo's Natural Herbal Ear Wash.

Natura Pet Products, Inc., P.O. Box 271, Santa Clara, CA 95052-0171. Phone: 800-532-7261. Manufacturer of Anmar, California Natural, Matrix, and Innova brands of dog food and California Natural Health Bar treats for dogs.

PetGuard, Inc., P.O. Box 728, Orange Park, FL 32073. Phone: 800-874-3221; in Florida, 904-264-8500.

Precise Pet Products, P.O. Box 630009, Nacogdoches, TX 75963. Phone: 800-446-7148.

Wysong Corporation, 1880 N. Eastman Road, Midland, MI 48642. Phone: 517-631-0009; fax: 517-631-8801; e-mail: wysong@tm.net; Web site: www.wysong.net.

Suppliers of Nutritional Supplements, Aromatherapy, Bach Flower Remedies, and Other Natural Products

All the Best, 2713 E. Madison Street, Seattle, WA 98112. Phone: 800-962-8266. Manufacturers of Enzymes Plus (enzyme supplement).

Animals' Apawthecary, P.O. Box 212, Conner, MT, 59827. Phone: 406-821-4090; e-mail: www.animals@bitterroot.net. Manufacturers of high quality herb extracts for animals.

Anitra's Natural Pet Products, Ltd., c/o Halo, 3438 East Lake Road, Suite 14, Palm Harbor, FL 34685. Phone: 813-854-2214. Web address: www.halopets.com. Manufacturers of Anitra's Vita-Mineral Mix, Anitra's Herbal Eyewash Kit, and other natural products.

Coastside Bio Resources, P.O. Box 151, Stonington, ME 04681. Phone: 800-732-8072. Manufacturers of Sea Jerky, a nutritional treat for dogs with arthritis.

Kyolic Garlic, Wakunaga of America Company, Ltd., 23501 Madero, Mission Viejo, CA 92691. Phone: 949-855-1776; 800-421-2998 (in USA); 800-544-5800 (in California). Manufacturers of high potency garlic in capsule, tablet, and liquid form.

PetNutrition, 191 University Blvd., Suite 252, Denver, CO 80206. Phone: 800-494-2659. Manufacturers of Good Gravy, a food supplement for dogs that contains beneficial bacteria.

Probiotics, 55 S. Main, Suite 122, Cottonwood, AZ 86326. Phone: 800-741-4137. Manufacturers of Flora Source (acidophilus supplement).

Zand Professional Formulas, P.O. Box 5312, Santa Monica, CA 90409. Phone: 310-822-0500. Manufacturers of herbal formulas for animals and people.

Suggested Reading, Videos, and Seminars

One of the first suggestions I give at my dog training classes is to read books by other trainers. When possible I also suggest attending their classes or seminars and watching their videos. Sometimes a concept that doesn't make sense coming from one person suddenly makes perfect sense when it is expressed in different words and shadings by another person.

So, whose seminars, books, and videos should you seek out? If possible, do it all. Even if you disagree with someone's methods, you'll still learn something—if only to confirm your own point of view and training ideals. This will give you even more confidence, which your dog will certainly pick up, and your training sessions are likely to improve.

I highly recommend attending seminars by Terry Ryan, Dr. Ian Dunbar, Dr. Pam Reid, Dr. Karen Overall, Karen Pryor, Ken McCort, Turid Rugaas, and Jean Donaldson. Also, I suggest any seminars offered by the Delta Society and the annual conferences of the Association of Pet Dog Trainers, where trainers and behaviorists from all over the world gather to share their knowledge.

Here's a list of books and videos I recommend for a starter library. They range from "how-to" to "why-for," that is, books and videos that present the theory behind the methods and the methods themselves. These books and videos can be ordered from Direct Book Service's Dog and Cat Book Catalog and Legacy-By-Mail, which are listed in Appendix C.

Training Books

Alphabetize Yourself by Terry Ryan (booklet), 1993, Legacy, P.O. Box 3909, Sequim, WA 98381. Phone 888-876-9364; fax: 360-683-5755.

Behavior Problems in Dogs by William E. Campbell, 1999, BehavioRx Systems (distributed by Direct Book Service; see Dog and Cat Book Catalog listed in Appendix C).

Clicker Training for Obedience by Morgan Spector, 1999, Sunshine Books.

The Culture Clash by Jean Donaldson, 1996, James & Kenneth Publishers.

Dog Behavior by Ian Dunbar, 1989, TFH Publishers.

Don't Shoot the Dog by Karen Pryor, 1986, Bantam New Age Books.

Excel-erated Learning by Pam Reid, Ph.D., 1996, James & Kenneth Publishers.

Games People Play . . . to Train Their Dogs by Terry Ryan (booklet), 1994, Legacy, P.O. Box 3909, Sequim, WA 98381. Phone 888-876-9364; fax: 360-683-5755.

How to Raise a Puppy You Can Live With by Clarice Rutherford and David H. Neil, 1992, Alpine Publications, Inc.

How to Teach a New Dog Old Tricks by Ian Dunbar, 1996, J&K Publishers.

Kinship With All Life by J. Allen Boone, 1954, 1976, Harper & Row.

Leading the Way to a Beautiful Friendship by Paul Owens, 1996, The Dogs of Operand.

Life Beyond Block Heeling by Terry Ryan (booklet), 1996, Legacy, P.O. Box 3909, Sequim, WA 98381. Phone 888-876-9364; fax: 360-683-5755.

Manners for the Modern Dog by Gwen Bohnencamp, 1990, Perfect Paws Inc.

The New Better Behavior in Dogs by William Campbell, 1999, Alpine Publications, Inc.

On Talking Terms with Dogs: Calming Signals by Turid Rugaas, 1997, Legacy-by-Mail.

The Puppy Primer by Terry Ryan (booklet), 1990, People-Pet Partnership, Washington State University, Pullman, WA 99164-7010.

The Puppy Report: How Reckless Breeding Threatens to Ruin Pure-Bred Dogs by Larry Shook, 1992, Lyons & Burford.

Superdog: Raising the Perfect Canine Companion by Michael W. Fox, D.V.M., 1996, Howell Book House.

The Toolbox for Remodeling Problem Behaviors by Terry Ryan, 1998, Howell Book House.

Training Videos

Paw-sitive Dog Training by Alan Bauman

Raise With Praise by Paul Owens, 1997, The Dogs of Operand

Power of Positive Training: Training Competition Obedience Basics by Patti Ruzzo

Clicker Magic: The Art of Clicker Training by Karen Pryor

Click and Treat by Gary Wilkes

Nonviolence

Cruelty to Animals and Interpersonal Violence, edited by Randall Lockwood and Frank R. Ascione, 1998, Purdue University Press.

Legal Issues

Dog Law by Mary Randolph, 1988, Nolo Press. Phone: 800-445-6656 or 650-549-1976. (A book on the legalities of living with dogs.)

Health Care

Dr. Pitcairn's Complete Guide to Natural Health for Dogs and Cats by Richard H. Pitcairn, D.V.M., and Susan Hubble Pitcairn, 1995, Rodale Press.

Food Pets Die For: Shocking Facts About Pet Food by Ann M. Martin, 1997, Newsage Press.

Four Paws, Five Directions by Cheryl Schwartz, D.V.M., 1996, Celestial Arts.

The Healing Touch: The Proven Massage Program for Cats and Dogs by Michael W. Fox, 1990, Newmarket Press.

The Natural Dog: A Complete Guide for Caring Owners by Mary L. Brennan, D.V.M., and Norma Eckroate, 1994, Penguin/Plume.

Pet Allergies: Remedies for an Epidemic by Alfred Plechner, D.V.M., and Martin Zucker, 1985, Very Healthy Enterprises.

Shiatsu for Dogs by Pamela Hannay, 1998, J. A. Allen & Co. Ltd, Distributed in the United States by Trafalgar Square Publishing

Holistic Health and Natural Living

Alternatives in Healing by Simon Mills, M.S., and Steven J. Finando, Ph.D., 1988, Plume/NAL Books.

Autobiography of a Yogi by Paramahansa Yogananda, 1946, Self-Realization Fellowship.

Health and Healing by Andrew Weil, M.D., 1983, 1998, Houghton Mifflin.

Love, Miracles, and Animal Healing: A Heartwarming Look at the Spiritual Bond Between Animals and Humans by Allen M. Schoen, D.V.M., 1996, Fireside Books.

Natural Health, Natural Medicine by Andrew Weil, M.D., 1990, Houghton Mifflin.

Nontoxic, Natural and Earthwise by Debra Lynn Dadd, 1990, Jeremy P. Tarcher.

Perfect Health: The Complete Mind/Body Guide by Deepak Chopra, M.D., 1991, Harmony Books.

Switched-On Living: Easy Ways to Use the Mind/Body Connection to Energize Your Life by Jerry V. Teplitz, J.D., Ph.D., with Norma Eckroate, 1994, Hampton Roads Publishing.

Aromatherapy and Bach Flower Remedies

The Aromatherapy Kit: Essential Oils and How to Use Them by Charla Devereux, 1993, Charles E. Tuttle Co., Inc.

Bach Flower Remedies by Edward Bach, M.D., and F. J. Wheeler, M.D., 1952, 1979, Keats Publishing.

Bach Flower Therapy: Theory and Practice by Mechthild Scheffer, 1981, 1984, Thorsons Publishers.

Magazines and Journals

Dog Watch, Cornell University College of Veterinary Medicine, P.O. Box 420235, Palm Coast, FL 32142-0235; Phone: 800-829-5574.

Dog Fancy, P.O. Box 53254, Boulder, CO 80322-3264.

Dog World, 29 North Wacker Drive, Chicago, IL 60606; Phone: 312-726-2802.

Front and Finish, H&S Publications, P.O. Box 333, Galesburg, IL 61402-0033.

Fetch the Paper, Pawprince Press, 815 Clark Road, Mablemount, WA 98267; Phone: 360-873-4333.

Off-Lead, Arner Publications, Inc., 204 Lewis Street, Canastota, NY 13032; Phone: 800-241-7619.

Pet Behavior News, P.O. Box 1658, Grant's Pass, OR 97526; Phone: 541-476-5775.

The Whole Dog Journal: A Monthly Guide to Natural Dog Care & Training, Belvoir Publications, Inc., P.O. Box 2626, 75 Holly Hill Lane, Greenwich, CT 06836-2626; Phone: 800-829-9165.

The Dog Whisperer™ DVD

Beginning and intermediate dog training
featuring Paul Owens,
author of the best-selling book
The Dog Whisperer

Fast! Easy! Fun! Results!

❖ Solve unwanted jumping, stealing, barking, pulling on the leash, digging, and chewing.

❖ Get reliable behavior without jerking, hitting, shocking, or shaking.

❖ Learn clicker training for faster results.

❖ Learn how to quickly wean your dog off food treats.

available at retail stores
everywhere
www.dogwhispererdvd.com
800-955-5440/818-623-0512

Index